FANATICISM IN
PSYCHOANALYSIS

FANATICISM IN PSYCHOANALYSIS

Upheavals in the Institutions

Manuela Utrilla Robles

Routledge
Taylor & Francis Group

LONDON AND NEW YORK

First published in 2010 in Spanish as
Convulsiones en las instituciones psicoanalíticas: el fanatismo en psicoanálisis
by Ediciones El Duende
Calle Estrecho de Gibraltar, 19, 28027 Madrid

First published 2013 by Karnac Books Ltd.

Published 2018 by Routledge
2 Park Square, Milton Park, Abingdon, Oxon OX14 4RN
711 Third Avenue, New York, NY 10017, USA

Routledge is an imprint of the Taylor & Francis Group, an informa business

British Library Cataloguing in Publication Data

A C.I.P. for this book is available from the British Library

ISBN 9781782200192 (pbk)

Translated by Estela N. Domínguez & Cora Lichtschein de Sueldo.
Revised for this edition by Caroline Williamson

Edited, designed and produced by The Studio Publishing Services Ltd
www.publishingservicesuk.co.uk
e-mail: studio@publishingservicesuk.co.uk

CONTENTS

ABOUT THE AUTHOR

Manuela Utrilla Robles holds a PhD in Medicine and Psychiatry from the Universities of Geneva and Madrid, where she also taught. She is a clinical director in Brussels and Geneva, and an adult, child, and adolescent training psychoanalyst. She has been President of the Madrid Psychoanalytical Society, General Editor of its *Revista de Psicoanálisis*, and Director of the Training Institute.

She has been an active board and senior member of the IPA and European associations, including the EPF, FEPAL, and SEPEA in Paris and ASUPEA in Switzerland.

She is the author of a number of books, including *Is Therapy Possible in Institutions? A Situational Study*, which has been translated into French and Italian, and *Dream Weaving: Parent and Child Psycho-analytic Encounters*.

FOREWORD

Ethical and moral issues have always pervaded human activity and human aspirations. Our field of endeavour deals with people's values, needs, and rights.

> A failure of ethics in psychoanalysis leads inexorably to technical failure, as its basic principles, especially those that structure the setting, are founded on ethical concepts of equality, respect and search for the truth. (Etchegoyen, 1999, p. 11)

As psychoanalysts, we have not learnt to detect the unconscious at work in our institutional relationships and the collusive forces permeating our relationship with our colleagues. Instead, we are accustomed to exploring our unconscious motivations and countertransferences in our work with patients and are much less aware of group pressures.

Dr Utrilla Robles addresses this conceptual lacuna in her second book of a trilogy called *Upheavals in Psychoanalysis*. It is a scholarly study in which the author explores a difficult subject matter that has been a taboo topic in psychoanalysis. She undertakes a serious study of the underlying arguments as to why psychoanalysts have seldom been able to live in harmony with each other. In a very lucid and systematic manner, Dr Utrilla Robles examines how a discipline, in this case psychoanalysis, can be manipulated to its detriment. She explains the disquieting processes that take place which impede the development of psychoanalysis. These influences insidiously infiltrate our ranks as a kind of arguing which should ostensibly enrich psychoanalysis, but instead deprives it of its creativity. For a discipline to prosper, it is necessary to have the freedom to air doubts, ask questions, raise hypotheses, and compare discoveries by sharing them with others, debating different positions to reflect on the discussions, and to change one's views if necessary.

This type of attitude stands in stark contrast to the kind of thinking that excludes and establishes norms to demonstrate how one is right in leaving no room for other ideas and creates research projects that cannot be refuted. The author's intention in this book is to study and shed light on these phenomena that have been considered taboo because of the secrecy surrounding them.

Dr Utrilla Robles asks the question, "What are the conditions necessary for this destructive behaviour to occur?" She notes that, as in all institutions, psychoanalysis is made up of various groups and individuals, and that these groups, under certain conditions, regress to more primitive ways of thought. These regressions, in and of themselves, have the chance to not be problematic if they can be identified and worked through. However, this process of working through problems is not always possible when dogmatic and fanatical forces are at work within the group. In order to describe fanaticism in psychoanalytic institutions, it is necessary to reflect on its roots and to study the history and development of intolerance and intransigence.

Of particular importance is the examination of the subtle slide from intolerance to fanaticism, which is facilitated when primitive modes of thinking prevail. Intolerance, which is based on primitive thinking, is characterised by an absolute certainty that is omnipotent and unquestionable. When it becomes a social reality, intolerance transforms into fanaticism. Fanaticism is characterised by dogmatic thinking, intolerance of differences, an eagerness to impose one's views, not tolerating free discussions, an inflated sense of self-esteem, and a feeling of omnipotence. Dr Utrilla Robles describes this state of affairs as *intellectual terrorism*, a phenomenon which, unfortunately, occurs all too often in psychoanalytic societies. How do the aforementioned aspects of human behaviour apply to psychoanalysis? How can a charismatic individual convince others to follow his ideas? First, he has to convince others with persuasive arguments presented in a forceful and passionate manner so as to not leave a trace of doubt of the legitimacy of his viewpoint. To stimulate interest, his ideas are presented in an intelligent way to highlight the implicit promise that it is his views alone that will bring about a change and improvement in psychoanalysis. These grandiose ideas appeal to insecure individuals, to the ones who feel discontented about their work, their relationships with their colleagues, and the institution. The forceful presentation of his viewpoint also seduces those who want to recapture lost ideals and those who want a charismatic leader to guide them. Once this alluring individual becomes a leader, he will use strategies to ensure he never loses his newly gained fame, to foster idealisation, and to sideline individuals who might become rivals by belittling them and criticising their work. The strategy employed is to wear out his critics by discouraging them. The followers of this individual are praised and are rewarded with important positions while the doubters are excoriated, viewed as poor souls who have been insufficiently analysed, as too sick to be analysed, or as liars who have an unanalysable character pathology. These conditions create an atmosphere of fear, suspicion, and persecution, resulting in a climate of intellectual terrorism.

What makes psychoanalytic societies so vulnerable to these disturbances? Psychoanalytic institutions are characterised by an inbreeding of their members, which creates special interactions that are beyond normal group interactions. The group discussions take place against a backdrop of rivalry, with its members trying to become followers so as to perpetuate this inbreeding and look for idealisations and admirers. Because of these conditions, regressive processes can become very intense, resulting in a slide towards animistic thinking and omnipotence in the group members. Dr Utrilla Robles calls this phenomenon *the fanatic cascade*. In many countries, psychoanalysis has functioned as a secret society where knowledge is the prerogative of the elders. This situation leads to a politicisation of psychoanalysis, which aims to maintain and develop regressive thinking in societal interactions by transforming the institution into an object of manipulation, which results in a situation where there is concealment of information, semi-clandestine decision making, and the use of aggressive strategies aimed at fostering the idealisation of hierarchy. Unfortunately, the result of this state of affairs is that conflicts of interests are resolved in favour of narcissism at the expense of principles. When omnipotence prevails over respect and dignity, a politicisation of psychoanalysis occurs. Leo Rangell has emphasised that the goal of psychoanalysis was the development of intrapsychic integrity, for the analytic attitude should be, in its very essence, a model of "relentless incorruptibility" (Rangell, 1974), a psychoanalytic perspective leading currently to the syndrome of the compromise of integrity.

Dr Utrilla Robles asks, "How can one fight fanaticism and deal with its fanatical constellations?" She answers by saying that none of us has completely abandoned our childhood omnipotent fantasies and that regressive tendencies lurk in all of us. When propitious circumstances emerge, our fantasies of grandiosity and domination can get the upper hand in our search for glory and admiration. The fight against fanaticism is possible but never final, because we must always be vigilant to detect, understand, work through, and try to overcome these disturbing and devastating phenomena.

The reader of *Upheavals in the Psychoanalytical Institutions: Fanaticism in Psychoanalysis* will be richly rewarded by this little gem of a book, which courageously tackles a subject that has plagued our institutions and generally has not received the attention it deserves.

H. Günther Perdigao, M.D:
New Orleans, LA- USA
Vice president of the International Psychoanalytical Association (IPA)

Introduction

How can we describe the multiple impressions which are gradually accumulated in our minds in the course of our passage through psychoanalytic institutions?

Like any other institution, the psychoanalytic institution is composed of diverse groups that, in turn, comprise individuals. Although every single person belonging to a psychoanalytical society has gone through a long and rigorous training, we cannot expect that their personal analysis or their psychoanalytical training alone will guarantee a permanent state of maturity of their psychic functioning. I am referring in particular to the fact—described by several researchers on group phenomena—that in certain group interactions there appear regressions to early phases or stances, to more primitive forms of thinking. These regressions would not constitute a problem for maintaining and developing the psychoanalytic science if we could at the same time *detect*, *work through*, and *elaborate* them. I believe these elaborations actually nurture psychoanalytic science, allowing its enrichment and diversification.

Regretfully, these elaborations are not always possible for a number of reasons. This can happen because their detection is difficult, or because some defence mechanisms that are too strong are hindering this awareness, or because resistances are installed as an obstacle to thought, and so on; or else because the extraordinary force exerted by fanaticism, as well as by dogmatism, prevent their elucidation.

For many years now, and profiting from the many works written on group and institutional problems, I have been able to position myself as an observer of certain disquieting processes that, in my opinion, are not only holding back the development of psychoanalysis but are also insidiously pervading it with the pretence of being postulations geared to its enrichment while they are, in fact, impoverishing and devitalising it.

When setting out to describe these phenomena, I have also had to consider the paradox that might arise if the attempt to unveil a problem contributes to hiding an even more pernicious one. Would describing fanaticism and dogmatism in the heart of psychoanalytic groups not be just another form of fanaticism?

The answer might well be in the affirmative if I were trying to show the authenticity of the descriptions, if I were convinced of their certainty, if I sought to persuade through my arguments, if I wished to transform them into unquestionable truths, into indisputable propositions. My position tends to be quite the opposite: it implies, rather, a certain feeling of sadness derived from verifying how a science that deserves so much consideration, that requires from us so much pondering and research to *keep it alive,* to defend its dignity and value, to return to it what it has given us—and it is certainly not little, since the analytic experience has transformed our lives, our way of thinking and feeling, our way of loving and our way of being in the world—can be manipulated.

To doubt, to question certain issues in one's mind, to proceed by way of hypotheses, to compare and contrast our discoveries sharing the findings, to *debate our positions*, to rethink and modify our points of view, all this is in contraposition with those postulations that pretend to exclude, to funnel certainties, to establish parameters designed to better demonstrate that one is right, not providing the slightest opportunity to introduce other ideas and thus establish allegedly irrefutable research proceedings.

Sadness, a feeling so close to mourning, enables me to interrogate myself, or better yet, not to stop questioning myself about the reasons behind all these issues that come to light when faced with these fanatical movements, and to try to find out whether they are also hidden in the depths of our own minds. And perhaps this is the reason why it is necessary to keep on reflecting and researching.

These subjects for discussion are vast, comprehensive, unattainable like the sky or the galaxies, but compelling to the point of arousing the feeling that perhaps they can contribute some knowledge, as in the expression used by Freud: "If someone speaks, it gets lighter" (Freud, 1916–1917, p. 407)

In my attempt to approach this vast subject, I have selected some examples and sequences of institutional experiences, but I have also resorted to other sources that can speak for themselves, such as the film *The Wave*; Stefan Zweig's excellent book *The Right to Heresy: Castellio against Calvin* (1936),[1] and the example of the fifteenth century Dominican reformer, Girolamo Savoranola. At the same time, I have compiled a series of reflections contained in other writings that I believe also address these problems.

It seems to me that Calvin's example, brilliantly described by Zweig, illustrates what takes place, though with less intensity, in some psychoanalytic institutions where psychoanalysis is idealised to the point of *deification*, that is, to the point of transforming it into the one and only therapeutic method, into a practice that can be applied to solve all problems, into a "common language" to be utilised as a unique language. This kind of psychoanalysis is used, in the same way that Calvin used God, to maintain the fanaticism of a few, and mainly that of a leader who works tirelessly to convince, employing any strategy and distorting the essential values of this science called psychoanalysis, which is the complete opposite of fanaticism.

After consulting the literature related to the subject I decided that most of the writings present a psychoanalytic study of fanatical personalities, placing emphasis on their pathology. In the excellent work of Sor and Senet de Gazzano (2010), we find a thorough research on this pathology that can help us understand the diverse perspectives from which this subject can be envisaged.

However, in this book, since it has been my aim to focus on the issue in the context of psychoanalytic institutions, I have restricted myself to addressing the problems associated to different situations, to the groups, and to some institutional processes.

From my point of view, it is not a question of putting the emphasis on pathologies that can be easily diagnosed, but of reflecting about certain situations charged with an array of different fanatical modalities. I shall attempt to better describe them by way of some examples.

The sequence is as follows.

I begin to develop my reflections in Chapter One, starting from an institutional experience that unleashes a series of investigations on what might be considered fanaticism and how it can can be related to dogmatism, a prelude of what we can term intellectual terrorism, which is so difficult to discern and even more difficult to understand.

There are innumerable works on fanaticism, especially following a series of events brought about by religious and political factions of fanatical characteristics. Situating fanaticism at the core of psychoanalytic institutions has demanded that I give serious consideration to its roots, that I try to study the mechanism of intolerance and intransigence, its history and development, and above all, the passage from intolerance to fanaticism, that subtle slide fostered by primitive thinking.

I most heartily wish that my colleagues do not find some of these examples offensive, since it is not my intention to refer to any person in particular. All the examples that I describe should be considered fictional, even when they are based on the real but partial sequences of some events. My conscious aim is to be able to study and elaborate these phenomena that, more often than not, are experienced in the shadows, as if discussing them were taboo, which causes them to persist and re-nourish primitive thinking. Is it, perhaps, that I myself also wish to oppose "conscience" to "violence"? Anyway, I hope not to share the tragic fate that awaited Sebastian Castellio, of being burned at the stake.

In Chapter Two, I address the difficult question of fanaticism in psychoanalysis, trying to elaborate on the problem of omnipotence that, to my mind, is the cornerstone of all fanatical tendencies. I will start by reflecting and examining the relationship between fanaticism and violence by using two well-known examples: Calvin and Girolamo Savoranola. In this chapter, the reader will find a description of their personalities and the ways in which they exerted their power in spite of the suffering they inflicted and the restrictions on liberties they imposed.

The descriptions we have of them are horrific, terrifying, shocking. For this reason, against these behaviours I set up a series of reflections I have called "A hymn to freedom", inspired by a paper on Freud´s essay, *Group Psychology and the Analysis of the Ego* (1921c), which offers—as the reader will be able to appreciate—a wealth of ideas and surprising explanations.

In Chapter Three, I deal extensively with the theoretical questions about group processes, mechanisms, phenomena, and dynamics that help us better understand the delicate fabric that groups weave within institutions, and analyse the paradoxes and other multiple psychic mechanisms that accompany them. In my view, the functions of the group leaders are of the utmost importance because, in general, their lack of knowledge and incapacity could go hand in hand with fanatical reactions that pervade institutional life, organising ways of functioning that distort the real sense of psychoanalysis, transforming them into a disorganised and destructive cascade of events.

The description of phenomena associated with fanaticism in psychoanalytic institutions based on real-life examples seems to cause a strong impression on us, and, therefore, I felt the need to address in the subsequent chapter the notions of respect and dignity and their loss as a result of what I call *the politicisation of psychoanalysis,* which I have tried to study starting from the notions of symbiotic community and identification with the aggressor.

All these particularities considered, I deemed it important to raise the question of whether it is possible to fight against fanaticism, and how to do so. By means of yet another example, we are able to explore the difficulties implied in this task, and the even more pressing need to continue elaborating and working through these phenomena and processes that are so complex and devious that they often escape our notice.

In order to carry out this psychic work, which requires incalculable thoroughness, we can resort to the model provided by psychoanalytic science, and, since I found it impossible to summarise and reproduce the entire body of work of the founder of psychoanalysis, I chose to refer to one of Freud's articles that, in my personal view, better describes the delicate psychic network we are confronted with. I have called it the Odyssey just to give it the quality of a long journey involving the interplay of ideas, hypotheses, and thoughts that can always help us better understand each other and resist the fanatical temptations that inhabit all of us.

Although most of my theoretical references are Freudian, because I feel more comfortable with them, I do not exclude other theorising.

I believe that, on an individual basis, psychoanalysts should work with the theories that are more in tune with them and about which they are most knowledgeable, without discarding the richness that others might embody. I consider any theorisation allowing us to think, advance, reconsider, and elaborate to be anti-fanatic.

Regarding the bibliography on fanaticism, I have found a great number of writings referring to the subject in more general terms and a meagre proportion having psychoanalysis as their starting point. The excellent works of Sor & Senet de Gazzano (2010), Javaloy (1984), Armengol Millans (2008), Bassols (1999) and Acuña Bermúdez (2008), among the most prominent, are in my opinion the most enriching, but they have their point of departure in theoretical positions that I did not wish to investigate here, since my main goal is not to research further on fanatic pathology, or to describe its dynamic and economic aspects, but to situate it in the everyday reality of institutional life.

I think the task of detecting the subtle fanatical processes that I describe in some of the examples requires that we adopt a prudent distance from the larger pathologies in order to appreciate the infinite array of purposes surrounding them.

CHAPTER ONE

What is fanaticism?

A dictionary definition of fanaticism characterises it as "an extreme or dangerous religious or political opinion, [or] an obsessive enthusiasm for a pastime or hobby" with "fanatical" describing the state of being "filled with excessive and single-minded zeal; obsessively concerned with something" (*Oxford English Dictionary*, 2007).

Hence, fanaticism could be described as a passionate and unconditional adherence to a cause, an excessive enthusiasm or persistent monomania regarding certain subjects, in an obstinate, indiscriminate, or violent way.

It alludes to any belief shared by several individuals or groups of individuals. In cases in which fanaticism outweighs rationality it can reach extreme levels, to the point of justifying the *killing, torture, or imprisonment* of human beings, and it can mask the unconditional wish to impose a belief considered beneficial for the fanatic, or for a group of fanatics.

According to its etymology, the word fanatic is derived from the noun *fanum*, which means "temple"; therefore, fanatic meant "belonging to the temple", and there was a time when it came to mean "protector of the temple". Later, it acquired the sense of a disproportionate abuse in the defence of religion. Thus, the notion of fanaticism was initially related to religion, but the term actually encompasses a larger semantic field. There are several kinds of fanaticism, and they originate in an affinity with a *person, a religion, an ideology, a sport or pastime,* among other sources.

Examples of fanaticism have occurred in the field of religion with the defence of dogmas, or the defence of sacred books or gods, or while defending a specific rational or irrational point of view. Religious individuals affirm that the difference between religion and fanaticism resides in the fact that the religious person views religion as a means to believe in or to know a deity, while the fanatic equates religion with god and considers it unquestionable.

For some authors, particularly for Sor and Senet de Gazzano, fanaticism represents a set of pathological processes. An extract from the cover of their book clearly expresses their stance:

> The authors attempt to discover the psychological roots of fanaticism by correlatively developing an innovative theory of play, a re-examination of the early bond between mother and child known as *reverie,* and an extensive enquiry into the latest theoretical findings on autism, arriving at their conceptualisation as inescapable precedents of fanatic behaviour. (Sor & Senet de Gazzano, 1993, translated for this edition)

Isolation and deterioration are key markers of this profound perturbation of thought and conduct. In this work, psychotic transformations are clearly and poignantly differentiated from the devastated, impoverished, and deleterious fanatical products. Dialogues and some extensive, unconventional biographical notes accompany these reflections. The authors point out, note, and sometimes give indications on how to try to protect the mind from fanaticism. They develop concepts on possible individual and group antidotes to fanatic contamination. The difficulties of such an enterprise are of enormous magnitude, because it deals not only with a negative presence, but with a subtractive bond that represents a void filled with infinite quantities of nothing.

A cursed language

In a meeting of psychoanalytical colleagues[1] one of the speakers announced unequivocally that a language spoken in the European territory was not an adequate language for psychoanalysis. When I heard this, I immediately doubted my ears. I thought it had to be my mistake and attributed it to a moment of distraction. I felt paralysed and shocked by such an outrageous statement. I looked around and saw some of my colleagues making gestures of disapproval. A sepulchral silence reigned in the meeting room, as if a bomb had suddenly fallen within the premises. Hastily, two colleagues took the floor. One of them rebuked the speaker, suggesting that, since he was the one who was always fostering the creation of research groups, he should organise one to provide valid arguments to back up this categorical statement. The other colleague said he did not agree with his strong stance and requested a retraction.

However, although there were many persons present in the meeting who were native speakers of the language in question, nobody else intervened. It seemed as though no one wanted to pursue the matter further, as if a menacing wave of terror had taken hold of the audience.

In all honesty, this was a very complicated meeting, as is always the case when not only scientific matters are discussed but, behind the apparent exchange of ideas, the real subject of debate is a series of complex group mechanisms with highly political purposes: Who is going to play a leading role? What are the forces at play in the conflict? Who is going to dominate? By way of which subtle mechanisms will alliances be created? Who will be the next leaders?

For, in fact, being heard and understood does not depend exclusively on what is being said; it also depends on who is supporting you or what is the hierarchical position you occupy in this long chain of shared interests.

In an environment such as the one described above, to voice your opinion is a risky move: you can make enemies; perhaps you might upset some individuals who might later have a bearing on your prestige; or what you say can be turned against you later. Thus, silence is a warranty of prudence and protection. A net of implicit preconceptions is woven: silence masks impotence.

However, this net of implicit preconceptions is never discussed or mentioned, as if it entailed an imminent danger. Probably this is also a result of the fact that its devious relationships are difficult to detect and often words to define them are hard to find. For many, this is a *substratum that is closer to the unconscious than to conscience*, and for others it is so to a lesser extent, because their conscious strategies have a goal: to become the most important personality/to achieve a place of prominence/to be the one that leads.

The attempt to understand these phenomena has led me to study, discuss, exchange views on, and try theoretically to elaborate what we can select from this undifferentiated magma.

While it is certainly true that by scrutinising just one violent and exclusive intervention we cannot conclude that we are witnessing a fanatic form of thinking, I found it sufficiently relevant to introduce this example as a starting point for the study of our subject.

What do we understand by fanaticism?

There are many works that focus on fanaticism from a psychological perspective: for some, what is particularly intrinsic to fanaticism is a longing for infallible security, as exhibited by those who, in fact, have strong feelings of existential insecurity.

Fanaticism is interpreted in this way by many researchers. For Adler, for example, fanaticism is compensation for a feeling of inferiority by refusing to admit that the dissenting party might be right.

Throughout his long and prolific career, Erich Fromm studied fanaticism and tried to explain it by associating psychology and sociology. His point of view is summarised in the title of his well-known book, *The Fear of Freedom* (1942), according to which all fanaticism is a regressive defence against the emergence of the sense of freedom resulting from the fear that this feeling provokes. In his opinion, fear arises as a response to anguished feelings of separation derived from the sense of helplessness experienced by the human being during childhood. To this, one should add an incapacity for love.

In addition, fanatics think they are the owners of the irrefutable truth. They state that they have all the answers and, consequently, they do not need to keep on investigating, searching, and questioning their own ideas by analysing what the criticism of others might represent.

Fanatics are, thus, characterised by their Manichaean spirit and by being the great enemies of freedom. It is unlikely that knowledge will prosper where fanaticism prevails, since fanaticism conspires against creativity. For Albert Camus, fanaticism is a form of destructive nihilism, as he posits in *The Rebel* (1953).

The consequences of the crystallisation of thought engendered by fanaticism are catastrophic. One of them is the departure from truth, since, in order to deepen our knowledge, we must be open to the discovery of that part of the truth that is present in others. This is a process that requires an intellectual humility unknown to the fanatic.

Another, yet more catastrophic, consequence of fanaticism is that it has always led to wars and terrible disasters. The intolerance practised by fanatics is the reason behind numerous social conflicts, wars, massacres, ethnic cleansing, and injustice.

Summing up, the features that characterise fanaticism are the following:

- *dogmatism*: faith in a series of "truths" which are not subjected to questioning or reasoning, and which are justified by their own nature or their relation to some kind of authority;
- *lack of critical spirit*: the free discussion or rational criticism of one's own "truths" is not allowed;
- *Manichaeism*: differences are considered in a radical way: no nuances or subtleties are admitted, and human diversity is conceived in binary terms: there are the good and the bad;
- *hatred of difference*: contempt for, and rejection of, everything that is not included within certain models or parameters;
- *eagerness to impose one's own beliefs* and to force everyone else to subscribe to them.

Coming back to the example mentioned earlier, I think it is important to provide further information on the person described. This person is known to be quite passionate, in particular when expounding his or her personal projects, which he or she defends in an authoritarian and irrefutable manner, thus gaining many admirers. Analysing this case we might easily detect some of the characteristics listed in the definition of the fanatic, for instance: "excessive and single-minded zeal". The term "excessive" might be the subject of debate, because what others find excessive, many of this person's followers consider interesting and really clever. But let us continue.

Although I have described tendencies towards fanaticism, their development and complexities, these often do not constitute indices that we can use to rapidly work out certain persons' traits. Even if we do detect such traits, we are very soon assailed by doubt: what if we are just exaggerating, or are simply unable to appreciate the force of that personality? What if we are actually jealous of the brightness that characterises many fanatics?

But yet another phenomenon occurs: a certain admiration emerges for the forcefulness of the fanatic's aims, for their absolute confidence in the validity of their ideas, their unfailingly loud tone of voice, all of which seem to personify authority. Since the human tendency for searching for ideals is very evident, and is coupled with the masochistic tendency inherent in all of us, certain psychic processes are created which enable fanatics to gain plenty of followers along the way to attaining their goals.

The history of humanity is full of examples of this kind, such as that of Savonarola, or of many other dictators. Now, if we could study them all (which is clearly beyond the scope of this book), we would realise that almost all of them have enjoyed a period of splendour, without anyone being able to stop them at the beginning of their rise to prominence, or to remedy the tragic consequences of their acts later on. It is as if this destructive force were unstoppable. The writer Stefan Zweig has contributed a brilliant description of this particular situation in his 1936 work, upon which I will comment later.

It is true that the diverse social and political movements founded by fanatics are not all alike, and neither may all the characteristics of fanaticism be found in scientific institutions. Yet, I believe it is important to try to investigate these fanatic phenomena that arise in the heart of the psychoanalytical institutions because they constitute potent forces that conspire against psychoanalysis.

The methods employed by fanatics might be of such a subtle nature that they can pass undetected: for example, the creation of research groups which are not aimed at debating ideas and proposals, but at deifying psychoanalysis, at measuring it, at obtaining verifiable statistics, at unifying and generalising it, even if this should require profoundly anti-analytical methods, where free association and evenly floating attention are metamorphosed into the recording of sessions, or even the production of video images of sessions in an effort to convince the audience by means of visible arguments.

In any scientific society, including psychoanalytic ones, we might find individuals with specific characteristics that everyone can recognise: personalities with high levels of narcissism, often decoded as arrogance, conceit, haughtiness, pride, acting as if they were the only intelligent and competent persons, the ones with the best ideas, which cannot be questioned or refuted, and the ones who truly know what they are talking about.

When they participate in scientific meetings, they often make reference to those whom they deem to be intelligent, thus losing their sense of reality, because they are implicitly calling everyone else fools, including all those who are listening to them.

So, what is happening? How can we understand the twisted mechanisms that might develop in psychoanalytic societies to the point of transforming the intrinsic freedom of psychoanalysis into a reductive and destructive way of thinking?

The Wave (Die Welle)

In April 1965, a history professor, Ron Jones, conducted at the high school where he was a teacher an experiment called "The Third Wave" (1976), by means of which he demonstrated that movements as repugnant as fascism and Nazism could easily recur. The results of the experiment inspired the writer Tod Strasser to publish, in 1981, his novel *The Wave*, which was subsequently made into a film.

Although it was not the first time that this novel had been adapted for the screen, it is worth mentioning that the 2008 adaptation was by a German filmmaker, Dennis Gansel (*Die Welle*, 2008), who dared to deal with events that, despite having taken place on American soil, directly attack the sensitivity of his countrymen with regard to their past.

Unbelievable as it might seem today that something like Nazism could happen again, this situation is precisely the starting point that professor Rainer Wenger—the high-school teacher in the film— proposes to his students when they discuss autocracy during school project week. The young students revolt and flatly and immediately discard the possibility of a recurrence of similar events, being fed up with the prejudices they are subject to because of their German descent. However, when the professor progressively incites them to show behaviour based on *principles such as discipline and unity*, the youngsters inadvertently become intoxicated by this new feeling of wellbeing, taking the experiment to limits that are beyond control.

The elements presented to them are basic: *a leader, a uniform (a white shirt), a distinctive salute . . . a group identity.* As a result, all the young misfits with families that ignore them, with low self-esteem problems, or simply with a low intellectual coefficient, find in *The Wave* something that brings some sense to their lives. Without them realising it, this fidelity to the group will turn into fanaticism; the same level of fanaticism that those who unconditionally reject them will eventually develop themselves.

For the purposes of comparing the phenomenon described in *The Wave* with certain work groups operating in psychoanalytic institutions, we could equate the uniform with the utilisation of a specific language, the distinctive salute with the use of clinical cases, and group identity with the belief in a deified psychoanalysis. The experience depicted deserves our closest attention.

If we put together all the characteristics of fanaticism described above, we will understand how their interrelation results in the creation of fanaticism. An overabundance of passion induces us to think of excess. In fact, the concept of passion alludes to perturbation, boundless affection, vehement desire, intense inclinations, and so on. We could observe that if all these definitions are associated with excessiveness, this is because they exceed the boundaries. Let us, therefore, retain the notion that fanaticism is closely related to the transgression of boundaries.

The other descriptive terms, "excessive" and "single-minded", making reference to the act of annoying, of exasperating, of infuriating—not to mention "extreme" or "dangerous"—are all aspects we can link to violence, so characteristic of sadistic impulses. With regard to the description of "obsessive enthusiasm" for a cause or a religious or political movement, we may associate it with idealisation and the creation of ideals.

The proposition of adherence to a cause can be considered from different aspects, such as adherence to drives, and the problem of attachment to persons that Mahler (1967) assigned to her concept of "symbiosis".

The concept of a force battling the feeling of freedom can have several explanations: for example, difficulties in maturing, libidinal fixations, the concept of psychic defences, and, above all, compensation for feelings of inferiority.

Claiming to have ownership of the truth shows a closer relationship to paranoid thoughts than to neurosis, and it can be equally associated with a lack of critical spirit and crystallised thought, which, incidentally, is a very revealing term.

Authoritarianism, hatred of differences, Manichaeism, and dogmatism are all products of this cascade of characteristics, which I shall refer to later in further detail.

The Wave provides other perspectives, too, which include the issues of leadership, groups, group identity, the search for a meaning in life, rhythms and strict rules, discipline and unity, the feeling of well-being, and the absence of the need to think. All of these represent problems that characterise groups and the regression to libidinal stages that have not been properly elaborated, in which, according to my hypothesis, the common denominator is omnipotence. I shall try to study omnipotence by exploring oral, anal, and phallic fantasies.

If we could integrate psychoanalysis into a unified theory and a universal practice, we psychoanalysts would experience a feeling of well-being, of absence of conflict. There would be no countertransference problems, but only a unified and permanent identity, a sense of belonging to the one and only discipline, an idyllic paradise. So, how should we interpret these drifts towards fanaticism in order to elaborate and overcome them?

Let us begin by analysing the roots of fanaticism.

The roots of fanaticism

One of the roots of fanaticism is intolerance. Intolerance is defined as the unwillingness or refusal to tolerate something. In a social or political sense, it is the lack of tolerance regarding the opinion and ideas of others, and, in a broader sense, it is defined as a lack of respect for any practices or beliefs other than one's own. For instance, in the domain of ideas, fanaticism is characterised by a steady persistence in sustaining one's personal opinion against the reasoning of others to the contrary. It presupposes a certain obstinacy and rigidity in the defence of one's intransigent ideas.

The consequences can be disastrous: discrimination aimed at groups or individuals (which can even lead to segregation and aggression) just because they think, act, or simply *are* different. The common factor of the multiple manifestations of this experience is the establishment of self-identity as a supreme value on the basis of ethnicity, sex, ideology, or religion, thus justifying the marginalisation of the other, who is different.

The constellations of intolerance can be numerous and vary in intensity. The most important cases in history, generally known to everyone, do not present the same intensity as the more subtle phenomena which we may encounter in any environment and which form part of our daily lives.

Intolerance of other people who are deemed different arises for a variety of reasons. However, it is always based on a difference from what is considered normal or correct by the judging party, who finds it impossible to accept the difference in the other, whether it is on the grounds of race, gender, culture, ideology, or religion. The most usual forms of intolerance are racism, sexism, homophobia, religious bigotry, and political prejudice.

Intolerance phenomena can be found anywhere. In psychoanalytical institutions, various attitudes suggest their presence: not respecting the way of thinking of other colleagues, a particular way of practising the profession or the theoretical framework, not tolerating arguments that differ from those one is used to, or even rejecting the ways in which others dress or behave. The list is endless.

Now, can we actually refer to a pathology of intolerance?

Psychopathic personalities

In general, we may state that psychopaths have a total lack of empathy and remorse, and, therefore, they relate to other people as if they were objects. They use others to achieve their goals and for the satisfaction of their own interests. They do not necessarily have to cause any harm, but if they do something for others or for an apparently altruistic cause, *they do it out of selfishness and for their own exclusive benefit*.

The absence of remorse and the objectification of others transform the psychopath into a rather peculiar individual in whom limits are distorted. The psychopathic personality is able to infringe social mandates despite being conscious of the majority of the common social practices, and can even display highly adaptive behaviour. For this reason, people with this type of personality can remain largely undetected. As a result of their egocentrism, these personalities focus exclusively on their personal gain or benefit, and when they do give, they are actually manipulating, or expecting to recover this investment in the future.

Other common aspects are: (1) an overrated perception of themselves, making them prone to megalomania and to an overvaluation of their own abilities to attain certain goals, and (2) a utilitarian empathy, consisting of an innate ability to perceive other people's needs in order to use this information for their own benefit; they are able to search the innermost self of the other person to discover his or her weaknesses and use these with a manipulative purpose.

Psychopathic personalities are not restricted to the highly publicised serial killer. Psychopaths can be charming, highly intelligent, and apparently receptive individuals. However, they will not hesitate to commit a crime when they deem it convenient, and will do so remorselessly. Most psychopaths do not commit serious crimes, but they will lie, manipulate, deceive, or harm people in order to achieve their aims without the slightest feeling of remorse.

Cleckley (1941) describes some characteristics of the profile of psychopaths as follows: superficial charm and good intelligence; absence of delusions or other signs of irrational thinking; absence of "nervousness" or psychoneurotic manifestations; unreliability; lack of remorse or shame; pathologic egocentricity and incapacity for love; general poverty in major affective reactions; unresponsiveness in general interpersonal relations.

Of the factors presented by a psychopath, as listed by Hare, Hart, and Harpur (1991), I mention the following:

- glibness and superficial charm;
- grandiose sense of self-worth;
- constant need for stimulation and proneness to boredom;
- pathological lying;
- cunning and manipulative behaviour;
- lack of any kind of remorse or guilt;
- shallowness of emotions and frivolity;
- lack of empathy, callousness, and insensibility;
- impulsivity;
- poor behavioural control;
- failure to accept responsibility for own actions.

In addition to these, I also emphasise those traits related to seduction, because I think this is a key issue in associating psychopathic personalities and fanaticism. One of the fundamental characteristics of the psychopathic personality is the innate ability to detect other people's needs. This mechanism is set in motion when psychopaths convince others of their complete dependence on them to meet irrational needs they cannot satisfy by themselves.

In order to seduce, psychopaths require the consent of the other person, and to obtain it they resort to persuasion and charm.

Intellectual terrorism

I shall narrate a story somebody told me some years ago about a situation that took place in a psychoanalytical institution, which I would not hesitate to describe as horrific. It involves a colleague who was highly recognised for her intellectual capacities and psychoanalytic knowledge. She was described by everyone as very clever, with an extraordinary power of seduction, capable of becoming one of the most charming persons on earth when she wanted something. Since she was endowed with great persuasion skills, her proposals were almost always accepted. Above all, she was able to perceive the needs of others. At the same time, she was manipulative, malicious, possessed exaggerated self-esteem, and she lied profusely.

Up to this point, the description could match that of many other persons, but what was particularly characteristic of her was that she could weave a fabric of terrible rumours that would cause people to be afraid of her.

When she appeared to be starting a new friendship, she would tell the person involved, with great excitement and a wealth of details, what other colleagues said about him or her in such a seemingly truthful way that no one dared to doubt her.

She would say something like: "This person told me that you copied from a book when writing your article and that you did not include the references", or "Z told me that you had spoken very negatively of M, that you had slandered him regarding his sexual tendencies"; "H says that you know what is going on with his wife and that you are telling everyone about it"; "R said that he saw you coming out of a hotel with a bad reputation"; "T is very pissed off with you because he says that you were spreading the word around that he is not only selfish but also a liar"; "P told me that you were propagating the rumour that he is a bad psychoanalyst who does not understand anything, and that his psychoanalytic practice is terrible". "Do not trust them," she would tell her new "friend"; "such and such are your enemies, and they are saying you are infringing ethics", and so on.

As a general rule, this analyst behaved in this manner with every person who would lend her their ears, and this was something that was really difficult to avoid, since she would approach her victims in such a way as to lead them to believe that she would reveal to them secrets they absolutely must know—that is, she aroused their curiosity.

In the institution, she would create an atmosphere of distrust and persecution counterbalanced by a bouquet of excessive compliments: "But everybody knows you are wonderful, very capable, very clever, a very good friend". And since the persons she used successively as objects to disseminate her lies did not dare to question their alleged "enemies", none of them knew about these rumours, except some who began to realise that what she was attributing to others was in fact what she herself thought.

This barrage of negative ideas about her colleagues would suffice to lead us to suspect great aggressiveness, intolerance, lack of respect, and many of the other previously described personality traits: glibness and superficial charm, overrated self-esteem, continued need for stimulus, tendency to pathologic lying, malicious and manipulative behaviour, lack of any kind of guilt or remorse, frivolous affective reactions and shallow emotions, lack of empathy, cruelty and insensibility, unrestrained behaviour, impulsivity and irresponsible attitude.

However, despite the fact that the institutional environment became increasingly awful, the institution in question appeared to absorb her terrorism, and all the parties involved forgot the insults to which they had been subjected. In fact, her absolute lack of guilt enabled her to meet with all those of whom she had spoken so badly with no remorse, and even when the rumours she had disseminated and the damage she had caused to many people finally came to light, some colleagues still excused her, arguing that she must be forgiven because "that was just the way she was". In this respect, the issue of masochism, always so alive in institutional relationships, must not be discounted.

We can see in this person all the traits of psychopathic personalities described above, and the story confirms that no one dared to denounce her methods.

In terms of fanaticism, we could say that the intellectual terrorism and the aggression to which she subjected her victims acted as an impediment to taking any action against her. At a later stage, when her great ambition placed her in higher institutional positions, she proved to be intransigent, intolerant, and dictatorial.

When reflecting about this example of a psychopathic personality accepted by the psychoanalytic institution, we have to enquire into the connection between psychopathy and intolerance that leads to fanaticism. There were still other traits: the dogmatism she used to defend her opinions, the strong impression she could make because of the fervour she showed during her interventions, her peculiar way of raising her voice while staring at her interlocutor, and her nods of approval when her potential victims spoke, aimed at deceiving them with regard to her real purposes.

In this example, her intolerance was not explicit, but it could be perceived in her constant speeches on the poverty of ideas in the institution, the absence of clever analysts, the need to elevate the intellectual level of its members, the need for scientific activities to be restricted to only the more prestigious members (whom she obviously selected herself), etc.

This case poses many questions about the excess of institutional tolerance as a way to counterbalance these levels of intolerance. However, can we understand what the source of this intolerance is?

The origins of intolerance

The polysemy of the term intolerance allows us to have a glimpse of the possible perspectives from which to study this trend, which could be considered the foundations of fanaticism.

The term intolerance is derived from the negative connotation of the verb *to tolerate*, and it may be referred to other related concepts, always in their negative sense: to support, to consent, to accept, to understand, to bear out, to pretend, to compromise, to condescend, and a long list of etceteras. Because of their common characteristics, all of these terms point out the difficulties in human relationships, so that we could infer that intolerance is at the antipodes of the concepts of society, of exchange and encounter, all of those things that bring to our existence a sense of being alive, because of the richness they provide.

The semantic perspective might lead us to many others: political, religious, sociological, historical, philosophical, psychoanalytical, phenomenological, etc. In these reflections, I shall refer especially to those of a historic, philosophic, and psychoanalytical nature, and I shall focus in particular on the latter, as well as on the possible connections among them all.

Due to its persistence throughout history, intolerance could be thought to be inherent to our human essence, and because of its resistance to change or modification, one might infer that its significance goes beyond political, religious, or sociological stances. From my personal point of view, and based on findings of previous works, I think that intolerance is part of what I have called historical fantasies, an assemblage of thoughts and imaginings which lack a sense of adaptation to the realities of the present, which were created in remote times and are still in force, and which persist throughout history with small variations, yet retaining an invariable core.

Let us suppose that in archaic times intolerance was necessary for the structuring of a human group and to institute differentiation in order to set both personal and group limits. Once the group became constituted, intolerance would no longer be needed, yet it would still persist as if it were, organising itself as a group fantasy.

However, intolerance is not a historical fantasy like any other. It represents the pillar that supports good and evil, the admissible and the inadmissible, understanding and the lack thereof, and so on.

In these reflections, and in an attempt to delve deeper into the roots of intolerance in order to outline the tree representing fanaticism and dogmatism, I will start with Manichaeism. My aim is that of observing the correlations between some areas of philosophical knowledge and psychoanalytical knowledge.

Although Nietzsche alerted us that methods come at the end, before engaging in a reflective process one should ponder, if only in an approximate way, the relationship between the method we are applying and the results of our research. A method which, to paraphrase Morin, detects and does not conceal bonds, articulations, interdependencies, and complexities; a method that mistrusts false clarities, not the clear and the different, but the obscure and the uncertain; not sure knowledge, but the critique of that certainty. This is a method which rejects abstract simplifications, which makes the simple complex, whith doubts and fights against idealisation, rationalisation, and standardisation; a principle of knowledge that not only respects, but also reveals, the mystery of things.

Thus, the method becomes a *school of mourning* (Morin, 1977), and this is why my approach, which will take Manichaeism and its possible roots in the *Babylonian Creation Poem* as a starting point, implies mourning for other perspectives, viewpoints, and trajectories.

From Enuma Elish *to Manichaeism*

As Heraclitus says, "And as the same thing there exists in us living and dead and the waking and the sleeping and young and old: for these things having changed round are those, and those things having changed around again are these ones" (Heraclitus, Fr. 88, in Kirk, 1954, p. 135), the state of being "asleep, while awake" will allow me to make an attempt at defining the roots of intolerance by proposing a relationship between the repercussions of the philosophical theory known as Manichaeism and group knowledge, which, in my opinion, revolves mainly around sacrificial practices.

Historians tell us that Manichaeism was founded by the prophet Mani in Mesopotamia, in the third century AD. Its central core is the rigorous distinction between two principles: the divine, which represents all that is good, and the diabolical, which encompasses all existing evil. These two principles are conflicting, irreducible, and independent from one another.

In the *Babylonian Creation Poem* (also known as *Enuma Elish—The Seven Tablets of Creation*) some of the notions found in Mani's theories begin to take shape. The poem begins like this:

> When in the height heaven was not named,
> And the earth beneath did not yet bear a name,
> (*Enuma Elish, First Tablet*, in King, 2007, p. 81)

These are inaugural expressions linking origins, the roots of many human trends, and words. But, at the same time, they suggest to us the relationship between what can be named and what cannot yet be named, what seems obscure and is not clearly perceived, or is sensed but still has no shape, or appears in one's mind as something undecided and unfinished, engendered in the abysses of our own mysteries. The abyss—*apsû*—derived from the Greek word *abyssos*, which we term abyssal; the abyss: the utmost depths from where the word comes to be.

The reading of the first tablet provides a glimpse of two different kinds of chaos: the original one, formed by aquatic chaos, or cosmic principle, a mass from which two elemental principles are isolated— Apsû, the primordial ocean, and Tiamat, the roaring sea. The mixing of these waters gives origin to the clouds and the serpents, which in turn form the celestial and terrestrial horizon, and, later, the great gods. In their quest to create new beings, these grand deities harass the couple Apsû–Tiamat and plan to destroy their offspring. One of them, Ea, will murder Apsû and transform him into Marduk, the central character in the Epic.

The second chaos occurs in the fight between the mother seeking vengeance and one of her children. After many vicissitudes, order is restored when Marduk, taking over the Tablets of Destiny, gains absolute power, and later, through his capacities of assimilation and his power, becomes a monotheistic symbol, the one and only great unifier.

In the Manichaean theories, a pre-cosmic primordial catastrophe produces a conjunction of *good and evil*, of light and darkness. A catastrophe resembling the beginning of the Epic Poem, which then continues,

> And the primeval Apsû, who begat them,
> And chaos, Tiamat, the mother of them both,—
> Their waters were mingled together,
> (*Enuma Elish, First Tablet,* in King, 2007, p. 81)

In this conjunction of good and evil of Manichaeism, good evolves symbolically into light and evil into darkness. Light and darkness can coexist, but the human being wishing to be good, full of light and wholesome, would have to restore the primordial separation and cast out evil, getting rid of it, forcing it out. All these procedures will later become exclusion and rejection patterns towards everything that is considered evil or bad.

Manichaeism expanded extraordinarily from Mesopotamia, reaching Northern Africa and, in the East, the Chinese Empire. It is interesting to note that, despite the persecutions it suffered from Roman and Persian kings alike, Manichaeism survived until the Middle Ages, and it was even promoted as a state religion in Turkestan and in a large part of Arabia until the advent of Islam.

Many scholars and thinkers adopted this doctrine, and it is well known that Saint Augustine followed its precepts for a decade.

Here, Heraclitus's idea (expression), which asserts that some opposites are essentially connected as extremes of a single process, illustrates the expansionist trends of a doctrine which, practised in an extremist fashion, could lead human beings along a path of intolerance and rejection of differences.

Even when the evolution of technology, and, in general, of all sciences, is clearly evident, a hidden desire to feel good still remains dormant in the heart of humanity, without ever considering that what is good for some could be bad for others, and that the exclusion of evil often goes hand in hand with destructive acts and conduct such as torture or the devastations that have inflicted, and continue to inflict, so much suffering on human beings.

Yet, since, in the Manichaean theory, the evil and the diabolic are associated, the worst atrocities and genocides are supported by this dichotomy between good and evil, between light and darkness.

To hunt down errors instead of establishing the truth

The idea of Edgar Morin, to hunt down errors instead of establishing the truth, will allow me to tackle the difficult question of truth and its correlatives: good and evil.

In philosophy manuals, goodness, as a transcendental property of the living being, is defined as the actual reality of the thing, in as much as it is beneficial for others and desirable to it. Just like unity and truth, goodness transcends all beings. For this reason, goodness and being are convertible. The argument that all beings are good comes from the premise that every living being has essential and constitutive perfections that are convenient for, and desired by, this individual, and are, therefore, good. It is interesting to note that this definition belongs to Saint Augustine.

Evil is defined as the opposite of goodness. Hence, it seems that if being and goodness are one and the same thing, then evil would be absolutely nothing.

To settle this difficulty, and given that evil *is* something, the kind of opposition operating between good and evil must be considered. We could think that if evil is not the simple negation of good, the relationship between the two is one of deprivation, so that *evil is the privation of goodness*, or of perfection in an individual suited to possess it.

As evil is dependent on goodness, its mission is good; therefore, we must look for the possible reasons that would explain its production: (1) the natural deficiency or imperfection of the cause producing the bad effect; (2) the cause does not apply, in a particular action, all the virtue it intrinsically possesses; (3) the action of a cause that is good in itself determines the privation of good in another individual; (4) a flaw in the matter that receives the action of a cause or the obstacles that the matter itself sets up against this action.

However, what might be of interest in our reflection is the categorisation of evil: absolute evil or evil proper, relative evil, or evil *per accidens*, which, although not in itself an evil, determines the privation of a good in another individual; intellectual evil, or the privation of intellectual perfection necessary for our understanding, such as error or ignorance; moral evil, or the privation of a good belonging to the moral order, that is, the deprivation of the rectitude of free acts or of their conformity to the moral laws.

It is true that these definitions have suffered modifications throughout the history of philosophy, in particular those introduced by Leibniz and Saint Thomas Aquinas. Some of the objections in Aquinas's *Summa Theologica* may illustrate the complexity of all of these definitions.

> Obj. 4. Further, Dionysius says (*Div. Nom. iv*) that evil has no cause. Therefore good is not the cause of evil.
>
> *On the contrary*, Augustine says (*Contra Julian i.9*): *There is no possible source of evil except good.* (Aquinas, 2007, p. 253)

These philosophical principles will help us to understand the relations between the historical, philosophical and psychoanalytical points of view. I have particularly highlighted some of the affirmations of Saint Augustine because, in my opinion, they were influenced by Manichaeism, as I have already mentioned.

Truth does not reside only in the conformity between knowledge and the thing, but also in its opposite, that is, in fallacy. And since, in logic, fallacy is an error in reasoning, what would be more heuristic than the pursuit of truth would be to hunt down the error. The error in the Manichaean doctrine, it seems to me, is the strict dichotomy between good and evil.

To revolutionise it all

In its early days, psychoanalysis represented a true revolution of ideas that has not yet ceased to offer great stimulus to researchers. Even though from its inception to the present day it has produced, and continues producing, novel ideas, it seems to be an inexhaustible source of possibilities for understanding the so-called intrapsychic world, as well as group, institutional, and cultural dynamics in general.

For these reasons, efforts are being directed increasingly towards differentiating psychoanalytic practice from the so-called applied psychoanalysis, that is, all developments or reflections made outside the psychoanalytical experience itself, which is solely referred to the encounter between analyst and patient.

From my point of view, this difference is essential to avoid falling into a confusion of ideas, always unfortunate in the course of research. In several of my writings, I have tried to reflect particularly on this phenomenon of the confusion of ideas, its trends, and the unconscious processes which often originate such ideas, following the three basic tenets posited by Edgar Morin: *idealising*, *rationalising*, and *normalising* (2001), but also considering the omnipotent desires of thought where conceptual boundaries are not respected.

An example might illustrate these ideas: however vast the theoretical knowledge achieved by a scholar of psychoanalysis (or of any other science, for that matter) may be, he or she could never pretend to be an expert in the matter without serious and rigorous practice to support this. Our inability to restrict ourselves with regard to the adequacy of the knowledge we possess brings about this effect of confusion, which could turn a psychoanalyst into a philosopher, and a philosopher into a psychoanalyst, or a historian, and so on.

Differentiation does not prevent contemplation of the relationships among these sciences; it even enriches them. Regrettably, in our fields of work, there are often rejections of these limitations and differentiations, aimed at nurturing the grandiose sense of knowing it all. This can be better illustrated by mentioning a prestigious professor who, when asked about the difference between the philosopher and the psychoanalyst, replied, "Differentiating bores me." To paraphrase Edgar Morin's lesson in this regard is also of great value: to reorganise our mental system; to re-learn to *re*-learn.

Based on our present knowledge of psychoanalysis, which is always evolving and uncertain, we can establish connections between the Manichaean doctrine and the *Babylonian Creation Poem*. These reflections deserve to be dealt with more extensively, but I shall restrict myself to summarising them in order to elicit some considerations on good and evil.

As postulated earlier, good and evil have brought, and continue to bring, problems to humankind, and, from a historical perspective, we might conclude that Manichaeism has represented the most coherent effort to propose a dualist solution to these problems.

However, from the psychoanalytic perspective, we could presume that there exists a relationship between what we call projection and the Manichaean tendency to dismiss the presence of evil in oneself and retain only what is good. Projection is a term that designates a mechanism of passage from the interior to the exterior, but, in psychoanalysis, a projection is a defence mechanism whereby the subject attributes to others the unpleasant thoughts that he cannot personally tolerate and that he interprets as reproaches coming from outside and addressed to him. This psychic device is one of the most commonly used, most precocious, and most resistant to psychic change, as is also that of projective identification, a term coined by Klein (1946, 1957) that has given rise to so many interesting works.

It is also true that many philosophical principles have been the source of inspiration for the Freudian opus: Empedocles' dualism seems to be an anticipation of Freud's theories. Empedocles, in line with Anaxagoras, accepts the *homeomeries* (similar parts), which Aristotle described as seeds or *spermata*, though he explains their combination as the forces he poetically describes as principles of friendship and enmity, which, in the field of science, are designated attraction and repulsion forces. It is through them that the elements unite or split to become a monad, or Supreme Being. (For more on this vast subject, see Barnes (2013).)

For Gressot, a psychoanalyst who has studied the Manichaean system in depth, it is possible to identify three psychoanalytic propositions:

(1) the Manichaean dualistic attitude that makes of the drive diffusion an ideal; (2) the dogmatic thinking and morals of Manichaeism that adopt an obsessive form; (3) the Manichaean conception of life that rests on fantasies of incorporation and projection (Gressot, 1953).

The creation of the world and the human being

Before reflecting any further on Gressot's three propositions listed above, let us go back to *Enuma Elish.*

The question of our origins is an issue that appears often in our attempts to theorise about our own psychoanalytic experiences. When Freud published his *Studies on Hysteria* (1895d), the only interesting critique of the book was that of Alfred von Berger, a professor of history of literature in the University of Vienna, who said, "We believe that the day will come when it will be possible to penetrate the inner secrets of the human personality . . . theory is no more than that kind of psychology used by poets" (Von Berger, 1896, translated for this edition).

The reference to the inner secrets of the personality implies origins that can be associated with the original chaos of the *Enuma Elish*. These references to chaos, disorganisation, capacity for unification, fate, and reorganisation can take us to libidinal stages, also known as genetic aspects of psychoanalysis, as well as to the notions of cleavage, splitting of the ego into good and evil (as developed by Klein, 1933, 1935, 1946, 1955), and to the integrative processes that organise the preconscious system, the artisan of associations of words and things based on latent thoughts.

Marduk the Unifier, the God and the Verb, the Word that becomes organised from the fog of the spirit, seems to represent that unification of the partial drives which allows for mental evolution.

Moreover, man's natural attempt to seek origins seems to contain an imaginative aspect of reparation: if we were able to find where and when certain problems originated, we would be able to solve them and in this way eliminate them, exclude them, cast them out.

Freud's writings also reflect this concern about the origin of fantasies, transforming them into original, primitive fantasies.

But the *Enuma Elish* epic can also suggest the idea of transition, of the intermediary, of the connections that might exist between the original and what follows, that is, the hypothesis on the consecutive psychic transformations of our personal history, especially of its organised repetitions, which are often organised as compulsions to repetition, transformations extensively researched by Bion.

The resemblance between origin and creation takes us to the psychoanalytic hypotheses of birth, whether the physical birth or, particularly, the birth of ideas and words.

The descriptions of the primordial chaos, the formation of the world, and the creation of the human being seem to have a point of encounter with those of the differentiation of the id in psychoanalysis, the constitution of an ego and a superego, and the creation of the verb—the word.

From the primordial chaos (the unconscious, the primary process?) we can isolate two principles—representations and affects. The list of comparisons is endless.

The dualism of man and nature advocated by the Manichaean system demands that which in psychoanalysis we would term the disentanglement of drives; that is, a return to the separation between life drives and death drives after having joined together—entangled— in order to structure thought.

The dualities between, above all, good and evil, but also between body and soul, light and darkness, the unconscious and the conscious, the rational and the irrational, etc., are all sources of innumerable anxieties, since tranquillity appears to originate in the fantasy of always feeling good, of feeling harmonious, lucid and perfect, conscious and rational.

According to Bion, this anxiety was the reason behind the great success achieved by Manichaeism during its lifetime, since the whole Manichaean postulate rests on the abolition of this anxiety.

The complex Manichaean organisation which, on the basis of that dualism, structures an entire life system, including deprivations and demands, in common with any other dogmatic system, constructs a philosophy of man aimed at granting him access to happiness. If, based on a psychoanalytic perspective, we consider that the unconscious is the domain of darkness, of the unknown, of the obscure, of that which threatens us, then Manichaeism excludes the unconscious and, consequently, the human being with no unconscious is not subjected to its threats.

We can ascertain that Manichaeism provided a certain coherence to the religious systems of the time, where chaos, magic, and the irrational led to confusion. But we must also consider the hypothesis that the sexual restrictions imposed by Manichaeism quieted consciences. Everything seems to indicate that Manichaeans were "visibly obsessed by preoccupations with sex and sexual fantasies, which had to be repressed" (Gressot, 1979, translated for this edition).

For Gressot, the mythical and moral conceptions of Manichaeism were impregnated with childish magical thinking, given the symbolism, syncretism, and animism that sustained them. In his description, we can find the whole gamut of fantasies in their libidinal stages: oral, anal, phallic, and genital. Above all, oral fantasies are prevalent. In numerous descriptions, oral integrations, incarnation by ingestion, oral fecundity, pregnancy through, and delivery by, the mouth, etc., are mentioned.

As we know, oral fantasies are the most confusional ones. Under the influence of such fantasies, a human being who has been eaten and digested by another transforms into the essence of this other one, loses his or her own identity, and there are no boundaries between one and the other. It is the most complete fantasy of omnipotence that exists, since one can transmute into a whole universe, the dominator and owner of everything that exists. Therefore, in the Manichaean descriptions, the inhabitants of the world of darkness devour everything they perceive and when there is nothing left, they devour themselves.

In summary, the oral stage is the non-discrimination stage *par excellence*, and for this reason we can infer that those who reject differentiations could be suffering from an oral problem. This matter is evidently more complex, because when the diffrences are not taken into account, the return to chaos or to the primary process signals that which, in psychoanalysis, is termed a formal regression,[2] that is, a regression of the mind to animistic thinking, also called magical thinking, a system of thought developed in great detail by Freud in *Totem and Taboo* (1913). In this work, Freud described animistic thinking as one of the great phases of human evolution that he classified as animistic, religious thinking and mature thinking.

Animistic thinking

This kind of thinking is closer to the primitive thinking described by Freud as operating under two beliefs: magic and sorcery. Magic consists in subjugating the phenomena of nature, while sorcery is the art of influencing the spirits. Both magic and sorcery form part of our unconscious fantasies and primary processes: primitive forms of thinking in which our wishes could come true without the need to transform them.

However, if we stop to reflect, this is actually an exclusively narcissistic relationship: there is no dominant and dominated, the dominated is part of the essence of the dominant. In this way, only one would exist, as in the fantasies of the oral stage in which everybody around, as a result of a cannibalistic fantasy, forms part of oneself.

The psychic evolution of a given individual from the time of his dependency on his parents until the time of his autonomy follows very complex trajectories which, none the less, share a common denominator: the capacity to elaborate, that is, the capacity to work through the psychic processes and construct associative processes arising from instinctive activities.

The diverse modalities that these psychic activities gradually constitute allow individuals to modify the progressive creation of the world and the people around them. Broadly speaking, these modalities are: identifications, the state of being in love, idealisations, and sexual activities, all of them activities we construct by means of our own phantasmatical capacity.

From an initially rather primitive creation based on omnipotence (the world belongs to the individual and he can dominate it) to the creation of a limited world (boundaries of the psychic world) the sense of maturity implies relinquishing omnipotence, relinquishing the fantasy of blending with others, of dominating and controlling them. It implies being able to seek alternatives to desires, not confusing oneself with others, not thinking for others, not pretending to dominate a group, and being able to establish relationships of exchange, which always involve respect for the other's dignity. This renunciation acquires a meaning through the elaboration of the process of mourning. As the Chinese proverb goes, "The greatest enemy of power is he who holds it".

This perspective of studying and analysing in depth the phenomena and processes of individuality entails the elaboration of identifications, along a path in which individuals would gain consciousness of their capacity for projection (that is, what they themselves project in the groups and in the institutions), of their need to emulate their elders (which is triggered by mechanisms leading to regression to the period of infancy), and to take them as role models (for thinking, understanding, being in the world, relating to others, etc.), and, later on, to be able to transform these partial features into operating functions (functions required in specific situations).

The trajectory of the constitution of the personal superego informs us of the level of maturity of the individual: that is, to be able to be with a group and within an institution without merging with others.

Now, this trajectory, which is difficult for any person, demands a true transformation of drive cathexes in terms of their aims and objectives. Instinctive activities that are restricted in their aims transform into currents of tenderness, inhibitions operated by successive desexualisations resulting from diverse mechanisms (regressions, defence mechanisms in general, and identifications). Thanks to this transformation of instinctive activity, an individual does not expect sexual compensation from another, but just to be loved tenderly. This implies retaining sexual desire (the psychic charge) and the object. While these transformations might give the impression of being great losses, nothing is actually lost, since the desire and the object are both retained.

Psychic functioning is, in fact, a phenomenon comprised of constant transformations, where no component part of the substratum is lost: drives continue to have their sources, their energies, their aims, and their objects. However, transformations are accompanied by feelings, fantasies, impressions, or sensations of psychic loss and gain— the loss of certain functionings and the incorporation of others. Some of these losses are accompanied by a sense of mourning, and mourning, in turn, by a feeling of having acquired the lost object for good; hence, the words by Henrik Ibsen (1866), "All that we have lost is ours forevermore"[3] seems to illustrate these psychoanalytical theorisations.

From intolerance to fanaticism

Intolerance arising from Manichaean stances may turn into fanaticism when, as the Chinese proverb says, it transforms into a social reality. And this is not just because intolerance represents one of the darkest aspects of humanity, but because it is based on positions of primitive thinking which themselves acquire a value of absolute and omnipotent certainty, without appeal.

When we contemplate the relationship that exists between historical, philosophical, and psychoanalytic perspectives, we realise that intolerance persists through the centuries as a force that seems to weigh against the idea of evolution and, although scientific progress seems to be transporting us towards a path of hope for humanity that we cannot even begin to imagine, we notice that certain views, certain human attitudes, are not modified in spite of our experiences. Would this be because we are unable to learn? Or, is it because we cannot realise that Manichaean views impoverish the development of the psyche? Or is it simply because we have not exhausted the possible hypotheses about its risks, and there are still persons who are convinced that fanaticism and dogmatism are the best tools of our thought?

However, we should also ask ourselves why we are so afraid of evolution, of change, of imagining alternatives that are different from those we are used to, of ceasing to practise the constant sacrifices to which our modern culture abandons itself, sacrificial rites that might not have the same components as those of times past, but yet retain in their core the same structures, the same components of suffering, revenge, exclusion, and segregation.

Faced with these discoveries, we have the impression that there is still much to be said and that it is most likely that we would need recourse to still more words in order to address those illusions that render ignorance a desire to know, and simultaneously render the desire to know a possibility for learning, in a perpetual movement of seeking and enquiry.

Good and evil, which have often been viewed as similar to love and hate and which, like them, represent two aspects that, viewed separately, would appear able to soothe the most archaic anxieties, are merely a part of the whole. They are contrasting pairs inserted in each of our ambivalent desires and provide us with the necessary strength to discover our future.

CHAPTER TWO

Fanaticism in psychoanalysis[4]

C omparing fanaticism to psychoanalysis seems to be an impossible task, because both are in complete contraposition and as far apart from each other as one can imagine. We should then wonder: how is it possible for persons who have gone through the personal experience of psychoanalytic treatment, and pursued a long and rigorous analytic training, to be able to embrace fanatic processes and mechanisms? Is not psychoanalysis ultimately a song to freedom that, as pointed out earlier, is radically opposed to fanaticism?

To these two questions even more considerations may be added: psychoanalysis has its limits, and no matter how many years of psychoanalytic treatment a person has gone through, he or she will not be "completely" analysed.

However, every person—psychoanalysed or not—can experience regressions, depending on the situations he is confronted with, and mainly within group activities, and since, in some regressions, a fanatic functioning might be present, we can, therefore, find psychoanalysts who unconsciously act in a way that shows all the components of the fanatic behaviour.

In order to have a better understanding of this situation, it would help to keep in mind that both the mechanisms and the processes associated with fanaticism are an intrinsic part of the development of the psyche. It is certainly true that if we were to describe the evolution of the psyche, from birth to adulthood, we would encounter at least some of the characteristics mentioned earlier: violence, tendency to primitive thinking, confusions and paradoxes common to fanatic thinking, a fixation towards libidinal states of early life stages, the difficulties of any developmental process that could bring about insecurity and fear, phobias, the discovery of otherness, symbiotic tendencies, separation anxieties related to highly invested objects, splitting, idealisations and other defence mechanisms hindering awareness, resistance to change, fetishism, perversion, and disavowal, among many others.

It is a fact that the long path towards maturity entails a slow journey full of ups and downs, and it is also a fact that undergoing psychoanalytic treatment does not guarantee the full psychic development required to complete that journey sucessfully. Psychoanalysis is a mental activity that is never completed and and continues throughout the lifetime. A person can be more evolved in some aspects but be trapped in others; hence, the great diversity of personalities that we can find in any psychoanalytic institution.

I think we are now in a position to address a major subject: psychoanalytic identity, regarding which we may assume that psychoanalytic capacity is not acquired once and for all; it must be constantly maintained by means of doubts, questioning, elaborations, and study.

As discussed before, from an openly primitive creation based on omnipotence at the beginning of life (the world belongs to the individual and he can dominate it) to the creation of a limited world (frontiers of the psychic world), maturity implies renouncing omnipotence, renouncing the fantasy of becoming one with others, of dominating or controlling others. It demands from individuals that they should be able to search for alternatives to their wishes independently of others, and not to think for others or wish to dominate a group; to be able to establish reciprocal relationships which always involve respect for the dignity of others. This sense of renunciation is obtained through the elaboration of mourning.

Instead of using the concept of maturity *per se*, we could speak of a certain level of maturity, since the notion of maturity could be close to the idea of perfection, and human beings are neither perfect nor completely mature. I am, therefore, referring to the sense of maturity, a psychic position that implies the predisposition to relativity and to doubt, to an attitude of permanent research in the face of the absence of certainties.

However, since everything related to the human psyche involves a conquest, this position is the result of a great deal of work and effort that we term elaborations: elaborations of varied infantile stages of the mind, from the most primitive (characterised by omnipotence, confusion, and the wish to subdue and dominate) to the most evolved.

In order to analyse these matters (omnipotence, confusion, domination, renunciation, awareness of otherness, which I have called respect for the dignity of the other) in greater depth, I need to rethink them (since all these subjects have been dealt with in numerous psychoanalytic writings and publications) in order to situate them within the auspices of fanaticism. This is necessary because I believe that in order for psychoanalysis to be able to evolve, some institutional behaviours, that is, the behaviours of some individuals who form part of an institution, should be the subject of further study and scrutiny, that they should serve as examples of what we are all prone to do under certain circumstances. In short, it is about unveiling and not concealing the problems that every psychoanalyst can encounter in the course of his or her activity.

The issue of omnipotence

The concept is so explicit that it hardly requires further elaborations. However, in order to progress in our reflections, we should make a distinction between fantasy and reality. To imagine that we are almighty, that the world belongs to us, that we can dominate and have supremacy over all things (that we are gods, in other words) is one thing. And to exercise this, to act it out, is quite a different thing.

Elsewhere (Utrilla Robles, 2010) I have described in great detail the question of acts and actings-out, and the transition from thoughts to acts and from acts to thoughts. I refer those readers interested in this subject to the relevant chapters in my book. For now, let us just retain the idea that our whole life is made up of a series of acts and that these can be the result of either a psychic elaboration arising from the reality principle or of a mental process becoming fixed in a regressive stage of our phantasmatical development.

Going deeper into the constitution of fantasies is beyond my present remit; nevertheless, I would like to mention here some of the main ideas presented on the subject by Rodríguez Daimiel, in a lecture delivered to the Madrid Psychoanalytic Society (1996).

Daimiel asserts that, from the structural point of view, the unconscious fantasy is a psychic construction ruled by the pleasure principle and driven by the fulfilment of desires. This corresponds to the Freudian definition of fantasy, which posits it as the truest expression of unconscious desire.

Topographically, it appears as a compromise formation between the preconscious and the unconscious, corresponding to Freud's conception of the psychic formation of retroactive causation, woven into the core of the preconscious and enforced by the unconscious.

From a metapsychological point of view, it is defined as an organised scene susceptible to being observed and featuring an action between a subject and an object in which the subject is always present, either as a participant or an observer, and where the object that initiated the fantasy is the privileged protagonist of the narrated scene. Consequently, in the unconscious fantasy, it is no longer a question of hallucinating a satisfaction that is identical to the one already experienced, but of satisfying in the psychic reality, in a hallucinatory way, the infantile sexual desires for an object, represented by means of images or of words, to compensate for their frustration in actual reality, when both realities have been identified. Therefore, what we are really saying is that sexuality is, in fact, psychosexuality.

Since psychoanalytic theory is based on the theories of a phantasmatic organisation, based in turn on infantile sexuality, I shall attempt to draw out from each libidinal stage what may be understood as omnipotence fantasies.

However, before elaborating further on this subject, I would like to make some observations on the so-called libidinal stages. Although every description of the characteristics of these stages suggests the notion that they are chronological moments in our existence, I envisage them rather as specific ways of thinking, as modalities of the structure of thought ruled and nourished by our unconscious desires constituted as fantasies, for which reason, at some point in our lives, fantasies belonging to different stages might coexist, depending on the level of transcendence of each libidinal stage and on each individual's capacity for regression.

Being all-powerful

Much has been written about the concepts of orality and psychosexual development, their sources and their objects, their instinctual aims and stages, but I am really interested in highlighting some aspects of their phantasmatic composition.

Elsewhere (Utrilla Robles, 1996), I have emphasised the idea that the concept of orality makes reference to unity; it depicts the realm of the self, since the main fantasy is that of incorporation. Everything that surrounds us is conceived as forming part of ourselves, mainly because in this phase there is no discrimination between the "I" and the "Not-I", since the model here is the one of the baby, who is not yet able to differentiate between what is internal and what is external, what belongs to him or her and what is part of the surroundings, or belongs to others.

Fantasies arising from these situations are of an exclusive, narcissistic nature: the world and oneself are conflated, resulting in the idea that everything belongs to us. This sense of belonging is also associated with other components. The so-called oral cannibalistic fantasy implies that if we can "devour" those around us and keep them inside ourselves, we can do with them whatever we want.

But these ideas are also intertwined with other fantasies: for example, the sadist fantasy, in which all violence against others will appear as natural, with no associated censorship or guilt. Eating is also associated with biting, dismembering, and destroying, ingesting and transforming it all into our own flesh. The craving, the urgent need and desire to possess, and the inability to tolerate delay encountered in this stage lead to frequent confusion between *being* and *having*.

Based on all these characteristics, we can already see that orality is the stage of the most genuine omnipotence, that is, the belief that everything belongs to us, that everything is ours; we can dominate and demand, with no limits or boundaries.

It is a well-known fact that this stage, the most primitive one and the one that contains the most extraordinary strength of our personality, persists in each one of us to varying degrees, ranging from the most fragile to the most vigorous, impetuous, brutal, enraged, and violent; from the most inconsistent to the most intense, terrible, invulnerable, and tenacious, depending on the level of maturity of our psyche, maturity that will be achieved through a certain degree of mental elaboration.

If we paused to describe the personalities of some dictators, rulers, or leaders who have employed aspects belonging to the oral phase in their attempts to subordinate and dominate others, we would realise that all the characteristics listed seem to fit them.

It is true that there are different degrees of power, ranging from the most violent and intrusive to that found in those who exert omnipotence from tortuous and more hidden positions, employing more perverse or twisted strategies. This has to do with the ability or otherwise of each human being, I would say of each psyche, to overcome some of the aspects described.

There are invasive personalities who can also establish affectionate relations, others whose desires to dominate can alternate with moments of guilt, others again that have established limits in certain activities but are unable to do so in their personal relationships. There is such a wide variety that it is hard to be specific; however, when confronted with any of these individuals, we can certainly identify many of these features.

Destructive power

The theory on infant development holds that a number of factors have been involved in order for the baby to pass from the oral to the anal stage: frustration, weaning, elaboration of fantasies involving a great energy charge, and the acquisition of language, which I have described elsewhere (Utrilla Robles, 1994) as prerequisites for fantasies to be modified, for the biological demands and the preponderance of corporal needs to be modified, and the predominance of corporal needs, since we should not forget that these stages are based on the needs of the body.

However, with regard to fantasies, these are subordinated to drive-impelled games and to the significance of noting that something (faeces) that comes from our innermost self can be lost, since we perceive how this element appears and disappears. At first, excrement might represent undifferentiated parts of the body, yet very soon the child is able to perceive their shape and consistency and might confuse them with other parts of their own body.

On account of the great variety of aspects associated to it, and their significance, this stage would deserve a thorough analysis, but I shall focus here on the problem of omnipotence.

I think—and this aspect has not been mentioned much—that the force exerted by children in order to defecate is linked to the belief that the faecal bolus represents strength, just as biting did in the previous stage. But in addition, the characteristics of its smell and, above all, the observation of the fact that those around the child find contact with it repugnant, rapidly turn these characteristics, in the infant's perception, into potential weapons for dominating others.

The violence associated with expulsion, and the effort of retaining, also contribute to imbuing this act with a semblance of power, which is inherent in omnipotence.

Although, in an initial phase of this anal stage, faeces might be conceived as gifts or offerings made to loved ones, since they come from inside the body, quite soon the matter of influencing, opposing, and provoking others moves to the forefront.

As in the previous stage, the sadistic drive to dominate can be very intense, but in this stage the sense of omnipotence becomes complicated: the other cannot be as easily manipulated as in oral fantasies, because in the oral stage the other does not exist as an independent entity, but as a part of oneself. Here, in the anal stage, the other is recognised as different and so, in order to oppose, compete with, try to compel him or her to do what one wants, to deceive or manipulate the other, more powerful strategies need to be employed. Anal sadism has been described as one of the most ferocious forms of sadism, one of the most difficult to bear and to offset.

For this reason, it has also been described as the stage of omnipotence *par excellence,* because it is also associated to bisexuality, homosexual desires, and narcissism. Bisexual fantasies arise because the rectum is an organ associated with the passage of faecal matter, because the faeces adopts the shape of a large penis, and because active expulsion can be interpreted as a masculine act. All these characteristics are associated to the active and the passive qualities that later will be re-signified as masculine and feminine.

Homosexual fantasies occur because the child can imagine that he is seducing his father with this passive attitude and, in this way, obtain his favours and be loved. Narcissistic fantasies occur for many reasons: because retention of the faeces might represent a triumph, a personal accomplishment that does not result in external praise but in internal sensations, and conveys a feeling of overvaluation and omnipotence; because the experience of expelling and retaining favours the awareness of antagonisms (big–small, good–bad, beautiful–ugly, etc.), so that the desire to become bigger and more powerful than adults can be felt as an omnipotent feeling; because the feeling of being loved by the parent of the same sex grants the illusion of exclusivity and of being the centre of the universe, so characteristic of omnipotence.

Grandiosity

From the point of view of psychosexual development, this phallic stage has been the subject of a great deal of discussion and research that would go beyond the remit of this work, so that I shall once again focus on the aspects related to the fantasy of omnipotence.

In this stage, the penis is conceived as an organ of omnipotence, so that individuals will be classified based on whether or not they possess this organ. At the same time, the lack of this organ in the opposite sex generates great anxiety, known as castration anxiety. The different kinds of anxiety associated with this are of paramount importance, not only for the evolution of the psyche, but also because they demand a redesigning of strategies aimed at the exercise of omnipotence. Exhibitionist tendencies are exacerbated, not only to suppress the anxieties by exhibiting force, but also to conquer, to be recognised and to be convincing, and, more importantly, because denial of castration anxiety can give way to a whole series of perverse procedures based on fetishism, such as feelings of magical omnipotence.

We can see all of these characteristics reflected in the examples of omnipotence that I shall present.

I should just add a few words to note that in the other stages, both the genital and the oedipal, the fantasies of omnipotence could have been transformed into fantasies of exchange, in which giving and receiving, sharing and (exchanging) constitute the fundamental elements.

We could say that omnipotence has been transformed into freedom of thought.

Conscience against violence

Stefan Zweig could not have chosen a more suggestive title[5] to study the intricate nuances of the issue of fanaticism. In his writings, with great skill, he presents a description of the characteristics of the initiation of fanaticism, of how it evolves, and the strategies that are employed to convince a large number of people, who are most probably not fanatics, to commit destructive and deadly acts.

We can find such descriptions in a multiplicity of works on the subject, but what is really original in Zweig is the contrast between this destructive desire, so subtle and sinuously expressed, and an opposite force that is expressed with so much energy that even fanatics fear it, and which Zweig calls *conscience*. How could such a proposal not be of interest to a psychoanalyst? In other terminology, we could speak of primary and secondary processes, and also of primitive thought as opposed to mature thought.

Zweig's writings help us to reflect on the problems of authoritarianism, tyranny, an ideology that resorts to terror to effect a tranquillising unity, the art of exciting the masses, the strategies employed to impose one's will, the sophistication in the brutality required to purify ideas and protect them from any harmful excitement, the misery behind reforms and the promises of beneficial changes, the attitude of victimisation behind which the desires of grandiosity and omnipotence are hidden, represented by divine symbols, the rigidity of convictions, opposition to any questioning or criticism, the use of sincerity to control others, the manipulation with firmness of those who doubt, the resorting to dogmatic positions with the purpose of splitting consciences, to try to make everything uniform, and the use of the ideas of purification and of a regenerative mission.

But what does all this have to do with psychoanalysis? I present an imaginary example to situate these issues within a psychoanalytical métier.

Let us imagine that a psychoanalyst begins to think that all theories should be unified in order to protect psychoanalysis, and that he or she also thinks everyone should express themselves in one single language, employing similar therapeutic methods, so as to achieve the uniformity of the psychoanalytic technique.

In order to accomplish this grandiose project, given that each psychoanalyst may work idiosyncratically, our hypothetical psychoanalyst starts thinking of strategies to carry it out. But first, he or she needs to convince others with persuasive arguments and his or her proposals have to be expressed firmly and leave no room for doubt.

The analyst in question will speak in a firm tone of voice, raising it from time to time, and will use intelligent ideas to capture the interest of the audience, yet these ideas will need to contain a promise of regeneration and change. He or she will try to show sincerity and passion for psychoanalysis and will have to formulate an apparently highly scientific project that includes the idea of unification (as we have seen when describing the oral stage). Thus, the first step in his/her reform would be unification.

But how can very diverse personalities be unified? By proposing a research project that would carry the imprint of something grandiose. This message of grandiosity can contribute to achieving the allegiance of the most insecure personalities (and even of those who are discontented with their practice, with their relationships with their colleagues, and with the institution).

In short, the most fragile personalities will be rapidly enthusiastic about recovering the lost ideals. But this will not only happen them, those who have doubts about the efficacy of their professional practice, but also to those who sincerely wish to change and even reinvent psychoanalysis, and to those who wish to recover ideals and to build idols, to find a leader who will conduct and guide them. Once our imaginary psychoanalyst has become a leader, the omnipotent narcissism of the creator of that unifying movement will start using strategies—conscious or unconscious—to hold this position forever. Thus, the long road towards an intellectual dictatorship, made up of multiple manipulations, persuasions, and arguments characterised by their certainty, will have begun. For example: psychoanalytic practice needs to demonstrate its credibility in order to be able to convince everybody of its usefulness, and to this end it has to be transformed into a practice in which competences can be measured and statistically verified. It has to be purified, that is, endowed with uniformity, for if something is to be measured, it cannot be variable.

This grandiose project demands multiple strategies in order to be perpetuated. Those who doubt will be threatened with expulsion; in religious terms, we would speak of excommunication. Those who support the ideas contained in the proposal will be promised important positions to keep them happy and grateful. However, we cannot ignore the use of violence exercised in the form of threats. For example, in this case, the threat of being considered idiotic or lacking intelligence, and of becoming a scapegoat of a group, and also the veiled threat contained in the well-known sentence, "You are either with me or against me".

Our hypothetical leader and other similar leaders are aware of the problems of any group, and use the group regressions to their own benefit, encouraging the ignorance hidden behind grandiose projects and the dictatorships of thought. But, how is it possible to keep a group in ignorance?

This can be achieved by several means, among which I wish to highlight concealment, the production of mysteries that are presented as inscrutable, the refusal to admit important problems affecting everyone, the creation of an atmosphere of fear, distrust, and persecution, and, above all, the establishment of the conviction that only one person is vested with a high degree of knowledge, the one that rules over all others, and that this person is the most intelligent, the most skilled, almost seeming to be a member of a unique race. In short, it is achieved through the idealisation of intellectual supremacy that only a few can claim to posses.

The system that is organised in this way is really simple. Those seeking peace and quiet can be happy that such a charismatic leader exists, thinks for them, decides for them, and safeguards the prestige and value of psychoanalysis. In this way, submission is transformed into something comforting that enables people to lead a better life, free from conflicts or problems. To avoid conflict becomes the primary aim.

Are these leaders invincible, given that they have to persuade everybody of their determination and truthfulness? As we shall see in the example of Calvin, they also resort to a strategy that is extraordinary because it provokes strong identifications in others: *victimisation*.

When someone with common sense opposes them and consequently turns into a feared enemy, the leader–dictator plays the role of a *victim* who suffers an unbearable affront. The leader will continually display his or her suffering, seeking to be comforted by followers, but mainly because in this way he or she exerts an extraordinary force of persuasion; as Zweig points out, one first has to have been a martyr in order to then become a hero of the masses.

As I will attempt to develop later in this work, when describing group processes, these can be divided into two categories: the constructive and the destructive; the elaborative and the regressive. The art of maintaining a group in a state of regressive thinking by employing progressive arguments requires a variety of procedures which are signified by distortions, slander, false rumours, perverse manipulations of all sorts, and fanaticism disguised as democracy. Do not all of these procedures remind us of fetishisation of thought?

In contrast to the fictional example I presented earlier, I will now explore two cases that existed in reality, which, because they are widely known and had a significant impact on history, are worth analysing: those of Calvin and Savonarola. From among the many dictators who have dominated the policies of their countries, the leaderships of these two strategists were intellectual dictatorships, reigns characterised by the imposition of ideas and cultural impoverishment that they left as heritage.

Both thinkers share some common features, as is the case with other dictators of the past and the present, and much can be learnt from them because, although their actions and personalities have no parallel in any psychoanalytic leader (in both cases the extreme violence of suppressing human lives was employed), perhaps the attempt to suppress or kill freedom of thought could be considered a crime like any other. But what they can teach us is that both Calvin and Savonarola were able to develop their strategies aimed at domination with absolute impunity and over many years, and no one was able to stop their deadly and destructive progress. Only when the extreme violence used by them reached a peak were voices raised against them, as if only excess could give rise to an opposition force.

Castellio against Calvin

In his book, Zweig begins with a quote from Castellio: "Future generations will wonder why, after so splendid a dawn, we were forced back into Cimmerian darkness" (Castellio, *De arte dubitandi*, 1562 quoted by Zweig, 1936, p. 1).

In the chapter "Calvin´s seizure of power", the author explains to us that a religious revolutionary and terrorist, named Farel, has succeeded in destroying and eradicating the Catholic faith and establishing reformed religion in Geneva.

Farel, who has a fanatic nature and a strong character, and is described by Erasmus as arrogant and audacious, exercises a true dictatorship over the masses. Short, ugly, and thin, the owner of a potent voice charged with an excessive fervour and violent overtones, he knows how to push people into an exacerbated state of excitement, because he can mobilise the hidden instincts of the masses, inflaming them on behalf of a final and decisive fight.

Before attaining victory, he had risked his life over a hundred times, had been arrested and persecuted, but the inflexible will of a man dominated by one sole idea broke down all resistance against him. He achieved success by using a considerable amount of violent and brutal methods. Zweig says, "A small but active minority can intimidate the majority by showing exceptional courage, and by readiness to use the methods of a terror—provided that the majority, however large, is slack" (Zweig, 1936 p. 30).

Yet, Farel is no more than a destructive revolutionary type that, with his power and his fanaticism, can do away with an obsolete regime, but is unable to build a new one. He can insult but not create, destroy but not construct.

After a swift victory, there follows a period of uncertainty in almost all of Europe, because Luther wanted to carry out a reformation, to reform ideas, to purify them, to transform them, and not merely deliver a fatal blow to the Catholic Church. And so Calvin arrives in Geneva at this particular moment in time; he was just passing through, but after a conversation he had with Farel, he devised the whole reformation movement that would follow.

But who was Calvin? A young man, twenty-seven years old, who sought refuge in Basel to avoid being arrested for defending the Reformation. He was a man from a good family, intelligent, cerebral, with an almost prophetic vision, a gifted organiser, and a tireless worker (if he was among us today, he could probably be described as working ceaselessly at his computer and sending e-mails to an extensive mailing list). He was aware that in order to unify the scattered reformist trends, a manual was needed, a book that would serve as a guide for the evangelist doctrine. And so he wrote the *Institutio religionis Christianae* (1536), which exerted a great influence on his contemporaries because of its implacable logic and its constructive energy.

Zweig describes it as follows: "Thus arbitrariness became dogma, and freedom led to the birth of dictatorship, while spiritual ardour was rigidly shackled" (Zweig, 1936, p. 36). At that early age, Calvin had already constructed an indisputable and immutable conception of the world, and even though he had to abandon the realm of thought in order to become involved in politics, his impressive ambition expressed itself in his becoming the unquestionable, omnipotent spiritual leader of the Reformation.

He would always act in the name of God, with whom he identified himself, but it was an unmerciful God who had to subjugate the whole world in any way he could, since the end justifies the means.

To acquire this power, he had to establish order and proceed in a methodical fashion. Order consisted in unifying all, prohibiting that which was not right (he was the one who decided what was right or wrong, good or bad), dictating rules and laws for all the citizens, demanding absolute obedience.

With a catechism of rules and recommendations, he wiped out in one stroke the Christian freedom advocated by Luther, based on a conception of religion as a matter of personal conscience. From the moment he arrived in town a single will ruled: his own.

With the goal of consolidating his aims, he developed numerous tactics. He presented his ideas with an apparent logic, in a simple and accessible way that could be easily understood by everyone. He dictated laws that could not be infringed under threat of imprisonment, he forbade any enjoyment, any manifestation of happiness, he inoculated feelings of guilt, but above all, he used violence and even brutality. In Zweig's words, he "throttled by brute force" (Zweig, 1936, p. 25).

Almost five centuries later, we could ask ourselves what this brute force consisted of, since it did not include physical torture (although this was not completely out of the question). It had to do with the psychological force of the fanatic with all the characteristics of oral omnipotence. Force fantasised as divine is inside the fanatic, he or she possesses it, it belongs to him or her, and others perceive it as an ideal. But since trying to take it away from the fanatic and incorporate it is too risky, the phenomenon of absolute admiration occurs, accompanied by an identification, as if the person were saying: "I know that I am not the dictator, but it is as if I were; all that he is doing I feel as if I were doing myself."

The psyche is predisposed to the exercise of violent acts. Sadistic drives can find easy expression, and since this fantasy is shared by a community of individuals—the majority—co-operation is also easier, as only the one who breaks the rules will be the scapegoat and could be expelled. In summary, brutality is the symbiotic force unifying all individuals of the mass and creating the fantasy of a perpetual and infinite well-being, since it has originated in divine sources.

The symbiotic double message is, "You are either with me or against me", and the grandiose nature of a supreme and divine ideal, nourished by continued messages of reform. Here, we can view reformation as an attack on more mature positions, on the characteristics of co-operation by agreement, on dialogue and consensus, on the sense of sharing and not possessing, of being and not of having, of winning after having lost, of effort, of elaboration, of going through experiences of mourning and humility, of critical thinking and acceptance of doubt.

Reformation can also be transformed into a search for persecutors who must be combated, and, as we all know, when in any community a witch hunt is unleashed, all the individuals that comprise that community feel united, bound by indestructible ties, and such unity provides a feeling of utmost happiness. Thus, we can understand better that this reformation can turn into a promise of infantile and regressive happiness that seems to be unquestionable.

I believe that Calvin was not aware of all this, but fanatical spirits act on primitive intuition. Their drives are closer to acting out than to elaborations, and in their regressions they find possibilities of producing grandiose ideals, such as an ideal of the ego that comes directly from the id: the ideal ego. When all the stages of construction of the psyche have been abolished, the fanatic will feed on strong, unshakeable convictions, on ideas which are close to paranoia and cannot, therefore, be appealed against.

Such a breakdown of the psychic processes necessarily has to be distorted by the multiple reality checks that all individuals experiment with. The psyche can split, proceed by way of disavowal, distort ideas, pervert itself, even manipulate its own thinking, and transform its beliefs into fetishes. It can become a robot that has lost all humanity and has only one mission: to dominate the world. For this reason, Calvin was not satisfied with subjugating Geneva; he tried to expand his reformation to all the Swiss cantons, and later to Europe, to finally conquer the whole world.

Zweig, with his usual mastery, describes the events in a proverbial way to transmit to us the tragedy we are witnessing.

When Calvin is confronted with the difficulties posed by the political authorities that are beginning to feel restless under his restrictions, he remains unaffected; in fact, he attacks. He mobilises his followers, who threaten opponents with redoubled intensity. Divisions appear in the Supreme Tribunal of the city, the Great Council of the Two Hundred, and terrorism starts to have its effects: citizens become accusers, denouncing one another, and generalised paranoia appears, similar to that experienced in other European regimes. Persecution expands to, and reaches the heart of, families. It is a reign of terror, and terror is fanaticism's best weapon.

In the different chapters of the book, a variety of strategies is described, among which is the discipline required to transform what is bad into good, since, for Calvin, man is an indomitable and brutal beast. What could better serve as a portrait of himself?

Now we see the appearance of Castellio on the scene: "The chief danger to an ideologist who has grasped the reins of power is a man who advocates a rival ideology" (Zweig, 1936, p. 94).

If we place the portraits of Calvin and Castellio side by side, the opposition the two men were to manifest so decisively in the mental field is here plainly symbolised in the domain of the sensual. Calvin's visage is all tension: it expresses a convulsive and morbid energy, urgently and uncontrollably seeking discharge; Castellio's face is gentle and composed. The former displays fury and fret; the latter, serenity. We see impatience *vs.* patience; impulsive zeal *vs.* persistent resolution; fanaticism *vs.* humanism. (Zweig, 1936, pp. 94–95).

After providing us with the biographical data of Castellio, the author depicts a man who is devoted to study and self-examination, a humanist, respectful of the ideas of others though a critic of the currents of destructive power. His intellectual ambition leads him to translate the Bible into French and Latin so the populace can know the truth, which was also the goal of Erasmus and Luther. Castellio was a young and wise man who devoted his life to the pursuit of independence, but since Geneva was under Calvin's dictatorial rule, and no book could appear without his consent, he asked Calvin for a meeting and then two wills were confronted: conscience against violence.

From that point onwards, Calvin would attempt to ruin Castellio´s career using specious, obscure, and devious arguments and advising against any appointment of Castellio. In turn, Castellio, whose conscience was clear, asked for explanations. The battle between concealment and the disclosure of truth, between manipulation and honesty, between one who was undoubtedly in favour of awareness and one who concealed his perverse strategies was bound to be a hard one, because the odds were against Castellio. It was power *vs.* humility, destruction *vs.* the defence of freedom.

What irritates a fanatic the most is that his or her ideal be doubted, and in order to maintain such an ideal, the fanatic will use devastating force.

Castellio, in turn, resorted to everything within his reach: he pleaded to the Council, inviting them to examine themselves instead of examining, judging, and punishing others. But his coherent and truthful arguments had no impact on a closed system self-contained in paranoia. He then decided to write, the best way to express his ideas of independence, but, through various manipulations, Calvin had already managed to have him, a respected and admired man, expelled from Geneva.

Two centuries later, Voltaire, referring to Calvin, would write,

We can measure the virulence of this tyranny by the persecution to which Castellio was exposed at Calvin's instance – although Castellio was a far greater scholar than Calvin, whose jealousy drove him out of Geneva. (Zweig, 1936, p. 112)

Calvin knew very well that he had precipitated his enemy into poverty, for he would not be able to find a position to secure a livelihood; he had banished him into poverty and indigence, and, to disguise his felony, he wrote to some friends encouraging them to provide Castellio with a job. In this way he presented himself as a generous man. But in spite of his plight, Castellio did not cease to denounce Calvin's intellectual despotism and his writings began to mobilise some consciences, for example that of Montaigne, who deplored that a wise man of Castellio's standing should have been so mistreated.

After years of deprivation and misery for himself and all his family, Castellio was able to obtain a poorly remunerated position as a professor. Still, his spirit of independence and his moral energy did not flag.

When Calvin sent an innocent man, Michael Servetus, to the stake for having doubted his theories, Castellio wrote this sentence, which was to become famous: "To burn a man alive does not defend a doctrine, but slays a man" (Zweig, 1936, p. 216).

Zweig's account of Servetus's life and death is daunting because it illustrates the cunning, the display of perverse mechanisms, used by Calvin to destroy the life of a man whose only sin had been to contradict his doctrines. Fanaticism can blind consciences, impose convictions, and coerce ideas: those who did not think like Calvin would end up killing in the name of some ideals that were not theirs, to the point of lighting the fire in which an innocent was unjustly executed.

Is it possible to understand why the humanists, the enlightened, peace-loving, non-violent men remained steadfastly silent?

In order to preserve his inner freedom, Castellio wrote his *De haereticis*, "The Right to Heresy", for most of Calvin's arguments against Servetus were related to his alleged heresy, but he was obliged to use a pseudonym, because he was banned from writing anything. According to Zweig, this book inaugurated an open battle against fanaticism by advocating tolerance. After using some of Calvin's own writings from the time when he defended the stance that no person should be persecuted for his or her ideas, Castellio patiently disassembled his thesis: Calvin supported his ideas on the Bible when talking about heresy, but in the Bible this concept cannot be found.

A heretic is a Christian who does not defend true Christian religion, but what is the true Christian religion? Heresy is not an absolute notion, but a relative one, and it is tolerance that might enlighten the spirits. Since, in each country or in each region, there are varied interpretations of the Christian religion, there would, in consequence, be very many heretics. Thus, the hunt for heretics is absurd. How courageous must be a man to write this in such a difficult time!

Personal convictions, Castellio argued, do not belong in the domain of a state or of a religion. He asked himself why there was so much hatred, so much wasted energy, so much persecution, and so much suffering? Responsibility for these horrible massacres, these barbaric persecutions dishonouring humanity, does not lie with the independent spirits who are the victims.

The only thing responsible for this deadly madness, this wild disruption of our world, is fanaticism, the intolerance of the ideologists, of those who want to impose their ideas at any price. Men imbued by such science, or, more correctly, by a false view of science, hold others in great contempt and develop pride, cruelty, and persecutory behaviour. Only tolerance can preserve humankind from such atrocities. In the world there is room for many truths, and if men so wished, they could live in complete harmony.

In the chapter titled "Conscience against violence", the author describes in detail the way in which the arguments Castellio wields to dismantle Calvin's doctrines have a strong impact on the conscience of the more moderate people and gradually gain ground. Calvin does not understand why citizens, instead of rejoicing at the death of a heretic, gradually begin to call him into question, him the grandiose, the owner of the truth: "Persons who are ruthless in the attempt to suppress the opinions of others are extremely sensitive to contradiction" (Zweig, 1936, p. 197). And even though Zweig does not lay emphasis on the strategy that the evil Calvin would employ, on reading his text, we quickly understand that there is a powerful weapon with which to recover power: *to play the victim*. Calvin writes about and proclaims how he suffers as a result of this situation; people should pity him and continue attacking the enemies of the fatherland. Once again, everything is permitted in God's name. Castellio then realises that it is not only fanatics who are dangerous, but also the fanatical spirit: what must be combated are ideas grounded in terrorism.

In the chapter "Violence disposes of conscience", we witness with infinite sadness the victory of perverse and increasingly twisted strategies: despite Castellio's clarity, the powerful truth of his words, and his freedom of thought, and despite the irrefutable proofs contained in his writings, which should move the most reticent spirits, these have no effect for the simple reason that they cannot be published. Calvin had banned Castellio's writings, a crime that remained unpunished, and in addition he mobilised a whole arsenal of political influences to attack Castellio, with the result that he was rendered impotent: "Against a reign of terror there is no appeal" (Zweig, 1936, p. 224).

Since violence has triumphed, Calvin feels his authority has been reinforced, and with the cynicism and brutality that characterises him, he manages to have Castellio threatened with legal proceedings. His premature natural death saved Castellio from a trial which would certainly have resulted in his being condemned to prison, exile, and probably the stake: at the age of forty-eight, his heart ceased to beat, tired of such an unequal and destructive fight.

In the chapter titled "Extremes meet", the author shows us how an entire population becomes accustomed to a theocratic rule: iron discipline, prohibitions, the absence of criticism, unique universal knowledge, self-control, coldness, and the absence of joy that characterise the Calvinist discipline transcend boundaries. Weber (1905) points out in his famous study of capitalism that the Calvinist doctrine of absolute obedience, ideal mediocre men, paved the way for industrialism, since it prepared the masses for the mechanisation I term *robotisation*, which was the origin of Puritanism.

Zweig rebels: "Forbidden, forbidden, forbidden; what a detestable rhythm!" (Zweig, 1936, p. 79) invades Europe, where "dynamic variety was sacrificed to monotony, and joy to a mathematical correctness" (Zweig, 1936, p. 261). Wherever Calvinism has passed, we can smell the death of intelligence, of humanism, of joy, of art, and of creative genius.

Yet, through a strange metamorphosis, the Calvinist system, which wished to restrain and suffocate individual freedom, created political freedom. Thus, through a wonderful transformation into the opposite, the countries most likely to suffer the consequences of that doctrine which destroyed humaneness were the ones that proclaimed the Declaration of the Rights of Man. There will always be a Castellio to rebel against a Calvin in order to defend the sovereign independence of any opinion against all forms of violence.

In this way, Zweig ends his book in May of 1936, but, unfortunately, a new, ferocious, terrible war is soon to strike humankind.

Girolamo Savonarola

The Italian known as Hieronymus Savonarola, or Girolamo Savonarola, was born in Ferrara, on 21 or 24 September, 1452, and died at the stake in Florence on 23 May 1498. He was a Dominican friar, a preacher, and a reformer who created and headed the theocratic dictatorship in Florence between 1494 and 1498.

He was known for his religious reformation and anti-Renaissance preaching. He vehemently preached against what he considered the moral corruption of the Catholic clergy, but without calling the dogma into question.

His early years (1452–1482)

Savonarola was the third child of a distinguished family from Ferrara, in the north of Italy. He was raised by his paternal grandfather,

Michele (a renowned physician and professor), who probably had some influence on his choosing to pursue medical studies. Initially, he studied at the University of Ferrara, where he obtained a degree in the liberal arts. He developed a strong interest in the Holy Scriptures and immersed himself in reading the works of Aristotle, Plato, and Saint Thomas Aquinas, in particular.

His anti-clerical inclination and his reformist traits are already present in his early writings. Thus, in *De Ruina Mundi* [On the Ruin of the World] (1472), a poem he wrote at the age of twenty, he denounced the corruption of society and the influence of lust and infidelity. It was at this stage that he chose his spiritual path, and his allegorical poem *De Ruina Ecclesiae* [On the Decline of the Church] (1475) displayed his contempt of the Roman Curia, which he terms in the poem, "a false, proud whore".

In 1475, he left his father's house and entered the convent of Saint Domenico in Bologna, where he worked as a tailor and a gardener before becoming a Dominican friar in 1476. He lived in conditions of strict asceticism. He immersed himself in theological studies and then left for Ferrara, where he taught Scripture at Saint Mary of the Angels Convent. In 1482, the Order sent him to the monastery of Saint Mark, in Florence.

He remained in Florence from 1482 to 1494, and spent the first years of that period devoted to ascetic practices and studying preaching techniques. At that time, he seems to have been reputed more for the former than for the latter. After a year's interval (1487), during which he served as "master of studies" in Bologna, he was sent to preach in several cities in the region. It was then that his true career as an inflexible preacher began, exhorting the masses to re-embrace the precepts of the gospels and not hesitating to confront the power of the Medici family. A poor orator in the beginning, his influence on the crowds gradually became stronger, and his harangues found an echo among some intellectuals of the time, such as the famous Pico della Mirandola, who adopted him as his confessor. In 1490, Lorenzo de Medici used his influence to have Savonarola sent back to Florence, in the hope that this would allow him to control the eloquence of his dangerous enemy.

At this time, friars in many regions became peddlers of indulgences. As a sign of his opposition to these sins, Savonarola withdrew from his secular studies and absorbed himself increasingly in the study of the Bible and the Church Fathers. In Florence, the monastery of Saint Mark had very strict rules (as demonstrated by his coarse clothing and the use of the cilice).

His fiery sermons would translate into an unprecedented social reform. Savonarola was not a theologian who proclaimed doctrines, like Luther or Calvin. He simply preached that the lives of Christians should include more goodness and fewer displays of excessive splendour. It was not a question of directly confronting the Church of Rome, but of correcting its transgressions. Savonarola preached against luxury, the pursuit of personal gain, the depravity of the powerful and of the Church, and the quest for glory. Soon, however, he denounced Pope Alexander VI and Rome as the incarnations of the anti-Christ.

Lorenzo de Medici, the virtual owner of Florence and patron of many Renaissance artists, was also a former patron of Savonarola. It has often been said that Lorenzo called for Savonarola on his deathbed in 1492, and that the friar did attend. According to the legend, on reflecting on his life and actions, Lorenzo refused to confess his sins to his priests and requested instead Savonarola's presence. As the friar was reluctant to attend, Lorenzo sent a messenger with the promise that if Savonarola accepted, he would do anything the friar asked of him, because he wanted to shrive his soul through confession. So he declared himself guilty of ill-treating Savonarola, and the latter imposed three conditions: that he feel true faith in God's mercy; that he give up his ill-gotten wealth; and that he allow the Florentines the opportunity to establish a democratic government. Upon hearing the third clause, Lorenzo allegedly turned his back to Savonarola, who then denied him absolution.

Lorenzo and his son and heir, Piero de Medici, eventually became the target of Savonarola's preaching. Then Lorenzo employed Fra Mariano, a popular preacher, to attack Savonarola from the pulpit. Yet, Savonarola had made such strong impression on the Florentines that, in spite of his eloquence, Fra Mariano was forced to resign after his first sermon.

Savonarola had predicted that a new Cyrus would cross Italy to re-establish order, and the impressive entry of Charles VIII's army into Tuscany in 1494 seemed to confirm his prophecy.

Theocratic government (1494–1498)

The Medici were overthrown during the French invasion in 1494.

Savonarola met the King of France, negotiated conditions for peace, and prevented the plundering of the city. Florentines were authorised by the King of France to choose their own form of government. Savonarola became the leader of the city. He established a political system he described as a "Christian and religious Republic". One of his first important decisions was to make sodomy, previously punishable by a fine, a capital offence. But he also introduced changes in the tax system in order to render it more just; he abolished torture, passed laws against usury, established a court of appeals, and a system to assist the poor. His chief enemies were the then Duke of Milan, Ludovico Sforza, who was an enemy of the King of France, and Pope Alexander VI.

Pamphlets urging violence against the Medici, whom he accused of being corrupt, contributed to the expulsion of Piero de Medici by the Florentines in 1495. Savonarola became the political leader of the city, where he established a theocratic dictatorship, proclaiming Jesus Christ "King of Florence". He gave young people guidance: adolescents dressed in white robes walked the streets encouraging Florentines to give money to the poor and contribute to charities, but they forced the people to do as they commanded, beating them up, committing all sorts of abuses, and practising torture.

In 1497, Savonarola and his followers held a "Bonfire of the Vanities". His groups of boys were sent from door to door collecting all kinds of objects associated with spiritual corruption: mirrors, cosmetics, images considered lewd, pagan books, gaming tables, fine dresses, nude paintings, books by poets considered immoral, such as Boccaccio and Petrarch. These objects were burned in large pyres in the Piazza della Signoria. Outstanding Renaissance artworks were lost in those bonfires, among them many paintings by Botticelli.

However, Florence began to become tired of Savonarola's excesses. During his Ascension Day sermon, on 4 May 1497, bands of youths rioted, and this soon became a fully-fledged revolt: taverns reopened and public gambling was resumed.

Imprisonment and execution (1498)

On 23 May 1497, Savonarola was excommunicated by Pope Alexander VI, and, in 1498, the Pope accused him of heresy, uttering prophecies, insurrection, and religious error. The trial by the Inquisition, as was the tradition, was carried out by the Dominicans, the same order to which Savonarola belonged. No proof of heresy could be submitted, except that he claimed to be a prophet guided by divine inspiration. However, Savonarola had lost all credibility, since he refused to be subjected to a confrontation his adherents demanded in order for him to prove his good faith.

He spent fifty days in prison and underwent two sessions of torture, one administered by the city of Florence and the other by a special envoy from the Pope. With a wounded body and his arms broken, he dictated in prison two interpretations of the Psalms.

On the day of his death, he referred to his abyssal misery at having declared under torture that he had not been divinely inspired. He repented of lying for fear of torture, and called upon the abyss of mercy to swallow up his abyss of sin.

Then he spoke with his two brethren, Domenico, who had contradicted him, and Silvestro, who was afraid to die. To Domenico, he said that during the night, it had been revealed to him that at the moment of death, he must implore the authorities not to hang him, but to burn him alive, as they should be happy to die in the way God had determined for them. To Silvestro, he said that it had been revealed to him that he (Silvestro) wanted to declare their innocence. However, as Jesus did not do so on the cross, neither would they.

The papal delegate then went to see Savonarola and his two companions to inform them that they had been condemned as heretics and schismatics, and had, therefore, been separated from the Church, militant and triumphant; from the Church on earth and the Church in Heaven. To this Savonarola replied that they may separate them from the temporal Church, but not from the church triumphant; that was not in their power.

The Pope's judgement consisted of a scroll in which he granted them plenary indulgence. They would be delivered from any punishment in purgatory, and their innocence would be restored. They were asked whether they accepted it. They were hanged and then burned in the same place where the bonfire of the vanities had been lit. Machiavelli was among the witnesses of the execution. The Medicis recovered control over the city.

Even after his death, Savonarola continued exerting an influence on those who had known him. A plaque still commemorates the site of Savonarola's death at the stake in the Piazza della Signoria in Florence.

For the Protestants, Savonarola was a very important person. Luther dedicated an inscription to him, calling him a forerunner of the Reformation. Others called him a prophet. Benedict XIV extolled the purity of his habits and the brilliance of his virtues; he was not afraid to say that the death of this great man demonstrated his mission, and that he had sealed with his blood the truth of his prophecies. And he went even further: the name Savonarola was inscribed in the catalogue of the saints and the blessed who are distinguished for their saintliness.

In these two men—Savonarola and Calvin—we may find all the characteristics I have outlined to describe fanaticism. Passion for their own ideas, which induces us to think about their narcissistic or "grandiose self", as Kohut (1971) described it; the fragile frontier between their beliefs and certain delirious aspects; their primitive thinking components, such as that of believing to be possessed by God's grace; omnipotence with oral and anal aspects, their vehemence, the wish to dominate others, a blinding ambition for power, the skill to influence and excite the masses, to become indisputable leaders and arouse admiration. In short, to promote and consolidate restricted and impoverished thinking based on unique and dogmatic ideas, a very particular way of thinking based on prohibitions, punishments, rigidity, severity, austerity, and sobriety that does not permit a free choice. The Puritanism in which a large part of the world was immersed based on these examples had fatal effects on the lives of many individuals condemned to expulsion from their communities and to undergoing unnecessary and cruel sufferings.

The harshness of certain customs and the Manichaean dichotomy of the classification of individuals into good or bad, acceptable or unacceptable, correct or incorrect, which entails contempt for differences and ill-treatment based on inequality, generate lack of respect and of acceptance of every person's dignity. It is, in sum, a question of advocating a racist division based on the belief that it is inspired by an omnipotent God, a supreme ideal that fanatics represent. In all of its meanings, fanatical thinking is closely related to paranoid thinking.

But all these characteristics, which originate in stagnation in the evolution of any individual with significant pre-genital fixations and defence mechanisms against sexuality, may be found in any person, especially in those who have been unable to constitute a sufficiently stable and evolutionary ego. Might all of us be fanatics?

Not all of us, because, following the teachings of the creator of psychoanalysis, who gives us a lesson on how we can fight against those regressive forces: knowledge, research, study, and the capacity to doubt and to accept the differences, might serve as vaccines preventing us from sliding towards animistic thinking.

The opposite side of fanaticism is freedom of thought, so let us see what Freud has contributed on this subject.

Group psychology, individual psychology: a hymn to freedom[6]

Each reading of Freud's work, *Group Psychology and the Analysis of the Ego* (1921c), lends itself to multiple interpretations, depending on a series of parameters, ranging from a certain ignorance in relation to his entire body of work to the scientific interests of the moment. It is for this reason that there are so many existing versions of this text.

In general, it has been understood by some as a relinquishment of the so-called intrapsychic stances and by others as an extension of psychic processes towards society. There are also some intermediate positions that combine the intrapsychic and the social, giving rise to increasingly anthropomorphic theories: society (understood as an abstract concept) would function like an individual, whence we might deduce a slant in which the concept is personified, that is, it becomes an individual, since reference is made to the social unconscious, or even to the social preconscious. We can also verify this slant in the opposite theorisations: the social and even the world would form part of our psyche, invading it and bruising it.

While it is true that each author draws the conclusions that seem to be more akin to his or her conceptions, and that it is not possible to put forward partial arguments without taking into consideration the entire Freudian *oeuvre*, the conclusions that Freud himself seems to have reached through his study of group psychology appear to broaden and tinge his theory of drives.

Freud described drives as compounds made up of several elements (sources, aims, objects, energies, representations, affects) (see for example, 1919a, p. 160) that link the intimately personal to the environment. The concept of drive is a relational notion.

This relational conception of psychic functioning takes on different nuances throughout his *oeuvre*. The concept of investment with an instinctual charge gradually takes on differential nuances in the course of his works, such as, for example, affectional bonds, identifications, ego-ideal, and/or the state of being in love, where we witness the emergence of different models enabling us to think about the complex relational fabrics, whether they involve relations between the different psychic instances or between individuals.

The numerous difficulties posed by human relations seem always to have been the object of Freudian research: with the psychoanalytic relation as his starting point, Freud studies some problems associated with groups and the masses. We very often forget this perspective. Apparently, Freud does not set out to study mass phenomena as a simple observer; rather, he *applies* his psychoanalytic knowledge, that is, he uses the teachings elicited from the analysis sessions to understand both the works of Le Bon and his own observations on groups.

This way of proceeding endows his conclusions with a value that differs from a philosophical or sociological reflection, or any kind of reflection based on other scientific parameters. Psychoanalytic parameters, I insist, are based on an individual conception characteristic of the analytic relationship.

Thus, throughout the reading of *Group Psychology*, we may notice how Freud gradually distances himself from the concept of collective soul to develop a theory that provides a broad perspective of the individual and his or her environment, as well as of the characteristics that the ego, subjected to stimuli that can provoke both its regressions or its maturation, might present. This evolution of his ideas resulted from his studying the psychoanalytical sense of mental contagion, suggestibility, libidinal ties, and the states of being in love, differentiating them from hypnosis to consolidate the notion of identification and the constitution of the ego.

The reader cannot avoid the impression that this trajectory constitutes "a hymn to freedom", since, if we envisaged an individual subjected to external forces, whose characteristics are predetermined by his or her history, without the capacity to react, his or her possibilities would be completely reduced and we would be in the presence of an individual who is a time robot instead of a person gradually acquiring internal freedom as a result of his or her elaborations.

In this way, and always resorting to the psychoanalytic perspective, Freud appears to break loose from the dilemmas contained in the controversies as to whether it is the external world that exerts an influence on the individual, or if it is the internal world that consolidates him.

The conception of an ego co-ordinating all the other psychic instances and being the creator of the external reality leads us to the notion of elaboration, a concept Freud develops in other works, but in the one we are addressing the possibility of becoming aware, through working through, of the participation of our psyche in regressive group processes is already present.

His famous phrase at the beginning of the essay, "and so from the very first, individual psychology . . . is at the same time social psychology as well" (Freud, 1921c, p. 69), broadens its sense towards the end in another phrase: how can the individual be separated from group psychology?

Now, then, Freud apparently attempts to define beforehand what he understands by the psychological group and its relation with the individual.

> Although Group Psychology is only in its infancy, it embraces an immense number of separate issues and offers to investigators countless problems which have hitherto not even been properly distinguished from one another. (Freud, 1921c, p. 70)

However, Freud seems to seek that which differentiates *and* links these two premises, individual and group, when he speaks of the group:

> It (a psychology) would be obliged to explain the surprising fact that under a certain condition this individual whom it had come to understand thought, felt, and acted in quite a different way from what would have been expected. And this condition is his insertion into a collection of people which has acquired the characteristic of a 'psychological group'. What, then, is a 'group'? How does it acquire the capacity for exercising such a decisive influence over the mental life of the individual? And what is the nature of the mental change which it forces upon the individual? (1921c, p. 72)

Before answering the question regarding the differences between individual and group, Freud reflects on suggestibility, hypnosis, and the state of being in love. Posing the question of the differences that exist between the individual and the group, he tells us,

It is less easy to discover the causes of this difference. To obtain at any rate a glimpse of them it is necessary in the first place to call to mind the truth established by modern psychology, that unconscious phenomena play an altogether preponderating part not only in organic life, but also in the operations of the intelligence. (1921c, p. 73)

These quotes subtly reveal that there is "something" that links individuals; at other times, he calls it a common denominator, and that "something" would apparently be unconscious phenomena.

If one continues reading, it becomes evident that Le Bon's conception is not the same as Freud's, for they have different conceptions of the unconscious. For Le Bon,

. . . the particular acquirements of individuals become obliterated in a group, and in this way their distinctiveness vanishes. The racial unconscious emerges; what is heterogeneous is submerged in what is homogeneous . . . the mental superstructure, the development of which shows such dissimilarities in individuals, is removed, and the unconscious foundations, which are similar in everyone, stand exposed to view. (1921c, p. 74)

In Freud's opinion, "in a group the individual is brought under conditions which allow him to throw off the repressions of his unconscious instincts" (1921c, p. 74).

Mental contagion, suggestibility, primitivism

Freud bases the effect that the group produces in the individual on three causes: mental contagion, suggestibility, and the identification of the group mind with the mind of primitive people (1921c, pp. 75–77).

The true dimension of mental contagion is not reflected in this essay, but it is in others. This may be understood on the basis of the theories on regressions, primary identification, and confusional fantasies (particularly oral and anal ones), which produce an impression of confusion between one and the others, but which, in fact, are, rather, individual psychic processes which any person may experience at a given moment without the need to resort to the group.

Freud conceives suggestibility as the loss of the individual's "conscious personality" (1921c, p. 75), which both Freud and Le Bon compare with the state of hypnosis.

As to its similarity to the mental life of primitive people, Freud refers to its characteristics: spontaneity, violence, ferocity, and also enthusiasm, feelings of omnipotence, and fetishist aspects. We also find these characteristics in the formal regressions that Fain (1966, 1982), has studied so exhaustively. They represent regressions to animistic thinking, which I have described in other articles (Utrilla Robles, 1996; Utrilla Robles & García Valdecasas, 1994).

On the other hand, in *Totem and Taboo* (1912–1913), Freud describes animistic thinking as one of the great phases in the evolution of humankind, which he classifies into animistic thinking, religious thinking, and mature (scientific) thinking.

Animistic thinking is closer to the primitive man's way of thinking, which Freud grouped under two tendencies: magic and sorcery. Freud establishes a clear difference between these. According to this, magic consists of subjecting the processes of nature to the will of man, and sorcery is essentially the art of influencing spirits. Both magical thinking and sorcery form part of our unconscious fantasies and of the primary processes: primitive methods of thought through which our wishes might be fulfilled without the need to transform them.

This primitive thinking has a common denominator, which is omnipotence, the result of a wish to dominate. The alleged power (and I say alleged because it is a fantasy) that we believe we have over people (as components of nature) leads to the consideration of only two positions in any relationship. This theory has been called binary or dyadic, since it implies a belief in a relationship in which a third party is excluded. But, most importantly, in this exclusive relationship of two, the other is only a product of our wish to dominate. This wish can be illustrated by the tendencies in certain persons to have people do as they wish, as if they were, in fact, the chiefs of a primitive clan to whom everyone owes obedience.

These fantasies are very frequent and they are expressed through acting-out in an attempt to control others, telling them what they have to do, making decisions about their lives, subjecting them to one's will, imagining that they may be influenced through making an impression on them, surprising them, dominating them. Generally speaking, these behaviours are characteristic of primitive minds that do not find in dialogue and negotiation, which are proper to more mature relationships, any incentive or any pleasure, because they do not admit the existence of differences and because their only source of pleasure is power.

Identification and situation

Before addressing some theories on identification, I will elaborate on Freud's perspective of libidinal ties, which we may understand through the concept of libidinal investment or libidinal cathexis.

Every human being is capable of making libidinal investments, since these investments form part of the essence of drives. Libidinal investments are, apparently, the strongest characteristic of our affective community.

Investment is an amount of psychic energy linked to a representation, a part of the body, or an object. The concept of investment is what helps us most to understand the individual, but also the generalisable, since that psychic energy marks the union between our psychic processes and our relationships.

Given that libidinal investments are common to all human beings, what differentiates them are their qualities and their forms of expression, which translate into different modalities of personal interrelations that depend on our individual history and our specific way of managing psychic processes.

What we may deduce straightaway from these reflections is that we cannot confuse that which is a common trait—libidinal investment—with persons. Having affects in common does not render us equal. That is to say, equality is not determined by our having something in common.

The psychic evolution of a given individual, from his situation of dependence on his parents to the situation of autonomy, follows complex trajectories, which have still another common denominator: the capacity to elaborate, that is, the capacity to become aware of the fact that one's instinctive activity has its sources in oneself, one's objects (which the individual chooses), and one's aims.

The diverse modalities that these psychic activities gradually constitute allow individuals to modify the progressive creation of the world and the people around them. Broadly speaking, these modalities are: identifications, the state of being in love, idealisations, and sexual activities, all of them activities we construct by means of our own phantasmatic capacity.

As I expressed previously and now repeat, given its importance, from an initial openly primitive creation based on omnipotence (the world belongs to the individual, who can dominate it) to the creation of a limited world (borders of the psychic world), the sense of maturity implies renunciation of omnipotence, renunciation of the fantasy of becoming lost in others, of dominating or controlling others; it implies being able to seek alternatives to wishes, not confusing them with people; not thinking for others, not vanishing into a group, and being able to engage in relationships of exchange which always imply respect for the other's dignity.

This perspective of studying and delving into the phenomena and processes of individuality entails the elaboration of identifications along a path in which individuals would gain consciousness of their projective capacity (what they themselves project on groups and institutions), of the necessity to imitate their elders (resulting from the unleashing of regressive processes towards childhood), of taking them as role models (in thinking, of understanding, of being in the world, of establishing relationships, etc.), and, later, of transforming the partial features of these models into operational functions (functions necessary in specific situations).

The trajectory of the constitution of the personal superego informs us of the level of maturity of the individual. That is, the capacity to be him or herself and be with a group and within an institution without merging with others.

Now, this trajectory, which is difficult for any person, demands a true transformation of the drive cathexes in terms of their aims and their objects. Instinctive activity inhibited in its aims transforms into currents of tenderness, inhibitions achieved through successive desexualisations, which are the fruit of very diverse mechanisms (regressions, defence mechanisms in general, and identifications).

Thanks to this transformation of instinctive activity, an individual does not expect a sexual compensation from another, but just to be loved tenderly. This implies retaining sexual desire (first psychic charge) and the object. While these transformations might give the impression of being great losses, nothing is actually lost, since the desire and the object are retained.

Psychic functioning is, in fact a phenomenon comprising constant transformations, where no component part of the substratum is lost: drives continue to have their sources, their energies, their aims, their objects. However, transformations are accompanied by feelings, fantasies, impressions or sensations of psychic loss and gain—the loss of certain functionings and the incorporation of others.

Hypnosis, the state of being in love and identification

In the trajectory between primitive and mature stances, Freud reminds us of the phenomena of hypnosis and the states of being in love: in both, "the tendency which falsifies judgement . . . is that of idealization" (Freud, 1921c, p. 112). Later, he will add that when we are in love, "the object is being treated in the same way as our own ego [so that] it is even obvious, in many forms of love choice, that the object serves as a substitute for some unattained ego ideal of our own" (1921c, p. 112) until the ego surrenders itself to the object, a surrender which might impoverish the ego. "In the case of identification the object has been lost or given up; it is then set up again inside the ego, and the ego makes a partial alteration in itself after the model of the lost object" (1921c, p. 114).

The difference Freud established between hypnosis and being in love depends on the position in which the individual places the object; whether the object is put in the place of the ego or of the ego ideal, as is the case of the hypnotist.

In this way,

> It might be said that the intense emotional ties which we observe in groups are quite sufficient to explain . . . the lack of independence and initiative in their members, the similarity in the reactions of all of them, the weakness of intellectual ability, the lack of emotional restraint, the incapacity for moderation and delay, the inclination to exceed every limit in the expression of emotion and to work it off completely in the form of action. (Freud, 1921c, p. 117)

According to Freud, all these features unmistakably represent a recession of mental activity to an earlier stage.

When Freud attempts to distinguish identification from the state of being in love, he says,

> In the former case the ego has enriched itself with the properties of the object; it has 'introjected' the object into itself, as Ferenczi (1909) expresses it. In the second case it is impoverished, it has surrendered itself to the object; it has substituted the object for its most important constituent. (Freud, 1921c, p. 113)

He adds,

Closer consideration soon makes it plain, however, that this kind of account creates an illusion of contradistinctions that have no real existence. Economically there is no question of impoverishment or enrichment; it is even possible to describe an extreme case of being in love as a state in which the ego has introjected the object into itself. (Freud, 1921c, p. 113)

Freud himself is aware of the fact that this distinction is open to objections. We must, therefore, ask ourselves what would be the essence of the situation of the ego, since, if the object is put in the place of the ego, this represents being in love, and if it is put in the place of the ego ideal, it represents hypnosis.

All these places are related to the individual's affective processes. However, if several people begin to imagine and their affections come into play, they may create situations which have common denominators for all of them: instead of transforming into thought, instinctive activity is acted out. These actings-out might be expressed orally or through different behaviours, and they might also be the product of an elaboration, or even represent simple psychic discharges.

Hence, the existence of such a wide variety of situations. But in any of them, we may verify the existence of common phenomena: expressions of affection (instinctive activity) and actings-out in the framework of a limitation process.

The limitation process, which I have already described elsewhere (Utrilla Robles, 1989) does not differ from elaborative processes in general, except for its form of expression: becoming aware of one's own limitations is a continuing psychic work, which Freud developed throughout his *oeuvre* and which culminated in his definition of the pleasure principle and the reality principle.

Other authors have also developed this, referring to the "skin ego", or "psychic envelope" (Anzieu, 1989, 1993), "theatres of the body", or theatres of the ego (McDougall, 1989), *"les visiteurs du moi"* [the ego's visitors] (De Mijolla, 1981), and so on. All these authors make reference to the mental capacity to expand through the imagination and through fantasies, to encompass the world and its components, delimiting oneself in others, losing the sense of oneself. Furthermore, also of withdrawing, of communicating with one's own ego, building one's own boundaries and work out situations that we ourselves can create, or to which we contribute through our own personal delimitations.

Delimiting–limiting one's ego would be two opposite poles in the constant search for harmony between our internal world and the world around us; two mental stances which may be thought and elaborated in groups and in the mass.

However, as Freud does not cease to repeat, acquiring limits (maturation) involves very fragile processes, since the pleasure principle seems to prevail over the reality principle. Tendencies to regressions, to a return to an expansive and devastating animistic–omnipotent thinking, would appear to be a constant force in each of us, always active, lying in wait for a weakness, or a failure, to become established as a demand which might never be met.

Freud warns us about this: what is not realised (when the sexual aim is not satisfied) persists with the same intensity, and, since it is impossible to achieve omnipotence (an experience of limitation will always exist), its intensity will persist over the years.

Group psychology and individual psychology

We may conclude that the expression "group psychology" seems to be more orientated towards Le Bon's conception than towards an individual mental functioning.

The question poses issues that might be endless, since, from a realistic perspective, it might be concluded that no person is alone and that the world is constituted by social beings.

Personally, I believe that the problem should not be framed in a fragmentary and totalitarian way, that is, the antinomy of individual and society.

For sociologists, for instance, the usefulness of their research resides in envisaging the individual under certain social parameters. Ethnologists would envisage an individual according to parameters of race or species. Psychoanalysts are concerned with an individual's mental world, with the aim of understanding when and in what circumstances his or her individuation processes are altered, and whether he or she can mature as a result of elaborations. Psychoanalysts are interested in what they believe is analysable, and we understand by analysable that which a particular person can elaborate.

Let us look at the conclusion that Freud reaches.

> We are aware that what we have been able to contribute towards the explanation of the libidinal structure of groups leads back to the distinction between the ego and the ego ideal and to the double kind of tie which this makes possible – identification, and substitution of the object for the ego ideal. (1921c, p. 130)

And, later, he says,

> Let us reflect that the ego now appears in the relation of an object to the ego ideal which has been developed out of it, and that all the interplay between an outer object and the ego as a whole, with which our study of the neuroses has made us acquainted, may possibly be repeated upon this new scene of action inside the ego. (1921c, p. 130)

To conclude, we might say that the possibility of transforming group psychology into individual psychology would consist of distinguishing the ego from the ego ideal and understanding its tensions, separations, and oscillations, which might provoke sensations closely related to losses (sadness), or to the feelings of triumph (which we might call "extreme well-being"), to extreme positions (in mania, the ego and the ego ideal are confused), and in melancholia (where there is an opposition–divorce of the two instances).

Since the ego ideal "comprises the sum of all the limitations in which the ego has to acquiesce" (Freud, 1921c, p. 131), "It was then, perhaps, that some individual, in the exigency of his longing, may have been moved to free himself from the group and take over the father's part" (Freud, 1921c, p. 136). Freud concludes, "The myth, then, is the step by which the individual emerges from group psychology" (Freud, 1921c, p. 136). The sentences that follow are particularly beautiful:

> The poet, who had taken this step and had in this way set himself free from the group in his imagination, is nevertheless able to find his way back to it in reality. For he goes and relates to the group his hero's deeds which he has invented. At bottom this hero is no one but himself. (Freud, 1921c, p. 136)

Freud refers to the capacity to symbolise as the capacity to render phantasmatic, and, ultimately, to the individual's elaborative possibilities. "Thus (the poet) lowers himself to the level of reality, and raises his hearers to the level of imagination" (Freud, 1921c, pp. 136–137).

It is not surprising that, after this explanation, he should describe the process of sublimation through which the individual acquires his or her maximum capacity for freedom.

CHAPTER THREE

Groups within institutions

P sychoanalytic literature includes a large amount of biblio-graphic material on group mechanisms and processes, based on extremely varied theoretical trends. In the UK, Argentina, and Spain (more specifically, Barcelona), Kleinian analysts (among whom I will only distinguish Bion, Jaques, Fornari, Bleger, Grimberg, Tizón, and Freixas) have contributed numerous studies and publications. In France, there are also publications from the Lacanian and post-Freudian schools: Anzieu, Kaes, Leclerc, Lefort, Mannoni, Oury, Tos-quelles, Mauco, Enríquez, Racamier, Lebovici, Talan, Lucas, Diatkine, Hochman, Cahn. There is a vast bibliography, but I will focus on a few examples: Foulkes (1975); Gómez Esteban (1997), James and Jonge-ward (1971); Nitsun (2000); Pichón Rivière (1987); Scheidlinger (1988); Yalom (1986).

This necessity to understand and theorise on individual experi-ences within groups is largely explained by the fact that psychoana-lysts, accustomed as they are to a relationship that involves two people (although we all know that this is not so, because the so-called third party(ies) are always taken into account), experience, when they are part of a group, feelings and affections which often disconcert them. We might say that this is what occurs in the best of cases, because in other cases they cannot even become consciously aware of the effects groups exert on their way of thinking. We have two very different positions: in the cases in which individuals are aware of these effects produced by the group, they try to elaborate them following the theorisations that are closest to theirs. The great problem is derived from the second example. When individuals cannot become aware of this fact, or they deny or repudiate it, then unconscious reactions result, which might have significant—not to say serious—consequences for the projects or the purposes of the group in question.

In an attempt to approach this difficult field of thought, the point of departure for my study will be the knowledge that we have of group mechanisms, although I will be forced to considerably narrow their descriptions on account of their extension and scope.

From the group perspective, many scholars have described the institutional issues, on which I shall not focus here because they will be the subject of the next book in this trilogy. I shall highlight only the fact that group functioning within institutions has some well-determined, specific characteristics that distinguishes it from that of other groups, and, within psychoanalytic institutions, these differences acquire a particular specificity, as will be confirmed in the course of this chapter.

In addition to the specific mechanisms and processes that are organised in groups within institutions, it would still be necessary to categorise in further detail the wide range of these groups, because each of them generates different processes.

Since we are used to the sense of "group" as applied in other works (Utrilla Robles, 1998), I have made the distinction between *groups* and *groupings*, for, if we abide by the definitions of group, when an assemblage of persons gathers together, they do not always exhibit all the characteristics to allow them to be called a group. A group implies the idea of having a common aim, a leader, and a setting allowing them to fulfil this aim.

Let us specify. We shall stick to the name of group to designate an assemblage of persons gathering together in defined spaces, at established hours, for an established length of time, and with an established frequency: the parameters that constitute part of the setting. In addition to this, the existence of a leader and a common consensus are necessary to make it possible to work on the aim.

The group model is the one provided by the therapy group, which meets all these conditions. In these groups, the aim is to elaborate and analyse the processes that are generated in the heart of the group. If we reflect about this, the therapy group is based, in turn, on psychoanalysis itself: a person makes a demand and a psychoanalyst responds, proposing a course of work that needs a setting. The difference in the therapy group is that the "patient" is an assemblage of individuals.

Within institutions, these therapy groups are usually rare, because the most common ones are the work groups, and those I have called *groupings*. The difference resides in that a work group has an organisation: an assemblage of professionals who wish to gather together with the aim of elevating their understanding of a problem and who devise the parameters of the setting guided by a leader. In groupings, there are no organisations established from the outset: a group of professionals may gather together without specifying either setting or leadership.

When Freud makes reference to the masses that have a director and those that do not, his descriptions serve as a model to illustrate the difference I draw between *grouping* and *group*.

The results are very different in one and the other: the role of the leader is to guarantee that the process evolves while safeguarding the opportunity for fantasies to be elaborated, as we shall see at a later stage. In groupings, that task is not possible, and group mechanisms may degenerate and produce increasingly alarming states of anxiety, confusion, and bewilderment.

But what do group processes consist of? Why is a leader necessary? What work must be carried out for the group to evolve?

Group phenomena, mechanisms, processes, and dynamics

The common denominator of all the different theorisations of group dynamics is regression: of the individuals comprising the group towards earlier stages of their libidinal development, and of thought towards animism, magical thinking, and omnipotence. These regressions may be understood by carefully examining *Group Psychology and the Analysis of the Ego*, which I presented earlier.

That said, if we consider a group as a situation created by the relations between several individuals, we might posit the idea that the excitement resulting from those interactions produces regressive phenomena which will depend on the level of development and maturity of each of the members of the group.

I think that the fact that an excess of excitement produces a regression does not require much explanation. Yet, it is not only a question of excitement but also, according to my hypothesis, of the perceptive incidents described by Fain (1966) in the production of dreams: to perceive in others traits that arouse our instinctive activity, in the manner of psychic alarms. Regressions on the one hand, and perceptive incidents on the other originate a mental functioning that manifests itself in the form of common fantasies, a sort of common denominator that only an experienced observer would be able to detect.

The whole phantasmatical spectrum that each psychoanalytic school contemplates might be described. Family fantasies characterised by jealousy and envy, by projective attitudes; unconscious fantasies of group idealisation; persecutory delusions and conspiracy fantasies; disaster fantasies; depression fantasies, and other disorganisation fantasies that create splitting; a search for rival groups and internal struggles with a whole array of destructive strategies.

This is the reason why it has often been stated that a group that is unable to work through this series of psychic constructions becomes psychotic, resorting to paradoxes and disrupting confusion.

The authors who consider group constructions as if a group constituted a collective unconscious describe group processes on the basis of the models of a person's psychic evolution: here, we might refer to the whole psychoanalytic theory, starting from the formation of symptoms, repressions, return, defence mechanisms, repetition compulsion, and disavowal, to name just a few well-known processes. In therapy groups, it is a matter of interpreting and working through all the pathological processes, adopting the model of psychoanalysis, as if the group were a person. Literature on group processes and dynamics is so vast that it would be hard to consider the conceptual scope and variety employed. I find this phenomenon interesting, since I do not believe it to be due exclusively to theoretical differences (bioenergetic, gestalt, systemic, philosophical, psychoanalytical, etc.), but also to a need to be able to think individual experiences within groups.

Since the earliest times, philosophers have been concerned with the phenomena originating in groups, but the proliferation of group theories appeared when Freud imparted his psychoanalytic theory and method and, in particular, following his essay, *Group Psychology and the Analysis of the Ego*.

From among all the works consulted, we can select some ideas.

- Each psychoanalytic school has studied group phenomena based on its orientation, and, consequently, we have numerous and diversified descriptions of such phenomena.
- As all of them utilise psychoanalytic references, we can consider the connection of many psychoanalytical concepts with the concept of "group" (the group ego, the group unconscious, the group pre-conscious, group transference, group defences, etc.), which give the impression of a certain amount of confusion between individual and group mental functioning (the group considered as an individual).
- The difficulties we might foresee in focusing on group phenomena as if the group were a separate entity, having its own nomenclature and its specific theoretical developments.

All these difficulties also result in the utilisation of four concepts: *phenomena*, *mechanisms*, *processes*, and *dynamics*, which designate the manifestations of an activity (phenomena), the ways in which they materialise (mechanisms), their development over time or forward movement (processes), and the power of their movement (dynamics).

These difficulties also depend on the lack of specification of the approach adopted by the researcher. Very often we do not know whether it is the phenomena in general (with reference to any group) that is being reflected on, whether it is small or large groups (and the denomination of "group" seems to encompass all existing kinds of groups) that are being described, whether the study is being carried out from the position of a leader or a participant, and also whether the researcher is utilising a single theoretical model or a combination of several.

Most of the works consulted seem to start from the authors' experiences as leaders of a therapy group; hence, those experiences seem to have served as the basis for the descriptions of group processes, a fact which must be taken into account when pondering the phenomena generated in other groups, particularly the training and work groups that are of special interest for this study.

Work groups: from paradoxes to organisation

Often, when thinking about organising a group to carry out a specific task, one does not take into account what might happen, because one starts from the notion that an assemblage of specialists is prepared to carry out a task. Let us suppose that within an institution the wish arises to create groups for the presentation of cases designated as clinical activities. The work seems easy to organise: it requires a co-ordinator, some presenters, and a group of participants. Since the task is to discuss the incidences of cure, everything seems to develop normally.

However, nobody seems to suspect that the fantasies of each individual will begin to be activated: those who wanted to take part have not done so, either because they have been afraid to voice their ideas, or because of shyness, or because they believe one has to be the best in order to take part. Those who do take part may be divided into two categories: those who are extremely satisfied with their contributions, and those who are discontented because they would have liked to have said something different. Let us suppose that the presenter/presenters felt dissatisfied because they have not managed to transmit everything they wanted to and because those who have taken part have attacked them unjustly. This atmosphere engenders ambivalent communications, narcissistic wounds, frustration, envy, jealousy, and other manifestations that occupy the field of experience. The aim was to achieve an exchange on scientific subjects, and what develops is an unconscious battlefield in which everyone might feel hurt.

What has happened? Has there perhaps been a regression towards animistic thinking?

Since the essential characteristic of animistic thinking is omnipotence, a notion on which I base a great majority of psychic processes that individuals develop and act out in institutions, it is important to be able to understand the relationship that exists between animistic thinking and the paradoxical system that represents the breeding ground where the relationships between specialists in institutions are created and intertwine. The so-called paradoxical communications often contribute to the creation of paradoxical situations, perpetuating some regressive relational characteristics that contain a high level of psychic suffering and impoverishment, where individuals feel trapped in blind alleys.

According to Freud, the three main evolutionary stages of human intellect are: the animistic, governed by narcissistic processes; the religious, in which object relations are created; and the scientific, which comprises the processes of maturation (Freud, 1912–1913, p. 88).

The essential characteristic of animism is omnipotence of thought. The animistic system, as I have already described it, is a set of beliefs, convictions, and actings-out that respond to the need to subjugate men, animals, and things, as well as to the need to subjugate the spirit. In order to implement all these subjugations, thought proceeds in accordance with certain variants, including analogy, substitution of the part for the whole, contagion, sublimated motivation, and so on.

Under evolutionary conditions, animistic thinking becomes sexless and later is repressed, becoming active once again when there are formal regressions.

As for paradoxical communications, the first to study them in their pathological and therapeutic sense were the inventors of the systemic theories of the Palo Alto School (Bateson, Haley, Jackson, Watzlawick, etc.), and subsequently many psychoanalysts have shown an interest in these communication phenomena.

Basing his work on Bertrand Russell's 1910 communication theory (his "theory of logical types"), Bateson conceived, in 1953, a research project aimed at studying in a systematic manner a broad notion of the nature, aetiology, and therapy of schizophrenia. The hypotheses of these researchers were based on the belief that schizophrenic persons are unable to differentiate logical types, which led them to observe the families of schizophrenic persons, deducing the existence of categories of messages, a sort of system of generally infra-verbal signals inserted in the verbal ones. Bateson terms these "meta-communications" (Bateson, 1972).

As has been studied by Cosnier (1989), in any society there are codes (gestures, tones of voice, rhythms, body language, etc.) that denote the characteristics of the messages. Since the meta-messages are imprecise, they might give rise to misunderstandings that might in turn degenerate into paradoxical and pathological exchanges derived from the abolition of the differences between interlocutors.

One of these messages, designated as double bind, is characterised by the following components: one of the persons involved in the interaction represents the victim, and those who issue the message must do so in such a way that a negative primary injunction is imposed upon the victim (for example, "If you do not do as I tell you, I will punish you"); a secondary injunction that contradicts the first at a more abstract level is also required ("Do not think I am an executioner"); a tertiary negative injunction is added that prevents the victim from escaping the dilemma created by the two former (through promises of love, for instance).

Discrediting and double binds contain more or less intense levels of irrationality that disrupt communication.

From the psychoanalytic point of view, we might understand this as a series of transformations of intents included in every message, which can lead us to think about the validity of unconscious processes. These might directly invade the preconscious system, in such a way that messages issued through words acquire contradictory characteristics.

The classic example to illustrate the essence of a paradox is that of Epimenides of Crete, who stated, "All Cretans are liars." He himself being a native of Crete, we might deduce that he is lying, but when he says he lies, he is speaking the truth at the same time. Thus, when he speaks the truth, he lies. Truth becomes non-truth, that is, a lie. As we may infer, the question is based on a global view (a totality: all Cretans . . .).

While paradox theoreticians prefer to speak of meta-messages, damaging remarks, or reversals, in psychoanalytic terms we think about the ambivalence of wishes, which might produce distortions in the narratives, in which we differentiate two contents: the manifest content and the latent one.

By manifest we understand that which is said; latent is what is implicit, non-verbalised, including an unconscious content, and which lends itself to a different translation depending on the person who listens.

It is not my wish to enquire into this fascinating field of the constitution and utilisation of paradoxical systems which has, indeed, also led to much confusion and abuse, but, rather, to connect paradoxical systems with the processes of primitive animistic thinking, which I believe govern and pervade the relationships between specialists within institutions.

Through these reflections, we might eventually better conceptualise the sense we ascribe to the concept of paradoxical situations.

Animistic thinking contains numerous paradoxes. Let us reflect on some of them: the Earth considered as a woman and sperm considered as the seed appears to correspond with a system of thought that uses analogies. When the primitive man ejaculates on the ground or practises sexual intercourse in the fields, convinced that he will thus render them fruitful, we may deduce that he is animated by magical thinking.

The firm belief in analogies is the consequence of magical thinking. We can base the difference between this magic and confusion on the notion of transitionality, since confusion condenses all the elements into a unit. Let us recall what I expressed when referring to oral and anal fantasies: these fantasies involve the issue of the absence of differences, since everything (beings, bodies, thoughts, or ideas) are contained within the same person.

Under the influence of an oral fantasy, an individual might come to believe that the world belongs to him, without his having had to do anything to possess it. The actions undertaken to maintain this state of complete omnipotence originate with the sole purpose of re-establishing the self-granted primordial right (I possess everything, and if it is not so, I must possess it by sheer force). We can present another version of this intent: whoever does not understand that I am lord and master of everything needs to be subjugated, invaded (bitten, eaten), swallowed.

The typical example would be the belligerent dictator who might kill in order to dominate, as in the case of Calvin and so many other dictators. Little does it matter whether human beings are alive or dead, what is important is to possess them. In any case, they are all annihilated beforehand and subjected to a single will.

In this fantasy (being the omnipotent dictator), the notion of complete understanding is excluded: the Other understands me as I understand myself. The absolute expression of the fantasy would imply the absence of the need to speak, since understanding has been predetermined beforehand. The other knows what I think in the same way that I know what he or she thinks.

Now, then, since I am everything (universe, world, countries, creatures, and things that populate nature and time), since everything belongs to me, when I speak it is with the aim of maintaining order, and not with the aim of communicating. In this system there are no paradoxes, since the confusion is complete.

The gaps in this system make it possible to understand the successive nuances that may be introduced.

We might say that this intentionality is present in all communications (I am completely understood: complete–total–absolute system).

The nuances in communication would reside in the possibility of tolerating certain gaps in this totalitarian system and maintaining the illusion of absolute possession. In order to be able to conceive these gaps (fissures, cracks, open spaces, etc.), we must introduce the notion of limits, a notion that seems to have originated in primitive thought.

If we revisit the example of fertilising the Earth by ejaculating on it, we must accept the possible existence of a hint of differentiation between the Earth and the individual. The omnipotent dictator will not have to make an effort to fertilise the land; even the cannibal demonstrates the existence of the difference between himself and his admired enemy.

In evolutionary terms, we would be referring to the differences between the ego and the non-ego, between internal and external space. If we paused to reflect on some of this subject matter, we would recall certain nuances of communication. The act of speaking with a person would arouse an unconscious fantasy that we might describe in simple terms in the following way: since my voice penetrates them, I can possess them, and if my ideas get inside them and I make them mine, I will know what they think. In this way, their thoughts and mine will be fused; we will understand one another completely.

Failure in this possession (which often appears in the form of a question—what is he saying?) might introduce concern and, at the same time, the wish to make an effort (as in the case of primitive man). Then the most important thing will be to make an effort to listen to him. Tolerance will emerge (a relinquishment of the wish to possess) thanks to the passive stance. This stance is already latent in the omnipotent system (I do not have to make an effort, be active, in order to obtain something). The passiveness implying a quantum of promise of obtaining that pleasure derived from possession is what will permit penetration—that is, listening.

What will be done with that which is listened to might turn out to be an adventure, ranging from the absence of recognition of the other to the greatest acceptance of the other. The majority of paradoxes are found in that space between believing that the interlocutor is accepted and the unconscious desire to dominate him or her. That desire will adopt very varied characteristics depending on each person's pleasure modalities.

When the desire of domination is associated with sadism, a conviction might arise that attacking, harming, and producing suffering are the best ways to understand one another.

Here, we might interpret understanding one another as laying out a net between two persons with the aim of their getting together and becoming an absolute unit.

Winnicott (1965a, 1971) has often differentiated between "in" and "with", differences that would indicate the possibility of abandoning the possessive system in order to have access to the pleasure of sharing, so remote from the first system that we could only liken it to light years.

Any example of institutional experiences might illustrate the paradoxical activity that becomes established in communications. According to the hypotheses I developed elsewhere (Utrilla Robles, 1998), when, in institutional groups, the fantasies that occur in the interactions between individuals are worked through, all the characteristics of animistic, paradoxical, and omnipotent thoughts tend to be *thought and not acted out*, so that the interactions turn out to be more mature and evolutionary.

It is true that when I say that those fantasies can be worked through, I am referring to a long trajectory amid indiscriminate and organisational processes, which depend on many factors, as I shall try to describe later, including the presence of a leader/group co-ordinator, his functions and his competences. *And it is precisely at this point that the whole fanatic system may be unleashed*: when, instead of helping the group to mature, the leader/co-ordinator keeps it in a regressive state in order to fanaticise it.

The functions of the leaders/co-ordinators

I begin by providing an example, which—as always—has been modified.

A colleague proposed the creation of some reflection groups based on clinical cases, in which the aim was that participants get to know each other better by exchanging ideas and opinions. He created a singular method: the participant who presented the case could not take part in the ensuing discussion, and the leader's only function was to facilitate the participation of the others. The setting consisted only of a series of established timetables. Given that his aim was to feel he was the creator of a new method (he idealised himself), he was not aware of the strange phenomena that occurred. Since participants could say whatever came into their minds, everybody raved, and since the person who presented the case could not contribute to rectify the situation, some participants literally invented the case, causing great anxiety in the group. The group became a battlefield in which to put right the other, and the aspect of strangeness was interpreted as an enriching experience. When the time to conclude the event arrived, the leader's function was restricted to adjourning the meeting. Many participants promised themselves they would never go though that experience again, but the inventor–leader continued to promote his groups with support from other members of the group who considered it very creative.

In this example, it would not be possible for us to refer to the larger context of fanaticism, as is the case in the example of the meeting that I shall submit later, but to aspects of fanaticism which could degenerate only if the experience became generalised. However, this allows us to pose several questions regarding the knowledge of group theories that leaders must possess, the setting they employ, and the aims they propose.

In order to address this subject, we will consider:

- the means (the knowledge they must have);
- conditions (the setting that may be utilised);
- the aims on which their activities must be based (elaborative);

Means

From the situational perspective, the leader must try to find a balance between his knowledge and the situation he is in, since it is not a question of mistaking a work team for a therapy group. Among the multiple confusions involving the functions of a leader/co-ordinator (functions which are always associated with fantasies linked to the exercise of power and control), the fantasy that the leader should become a saving Messiah, a fantasy rationalised through that of the group therapist, is the more generalised one: the leader should fix any problem, avoid difficulties, and, if any arise, find adequate solutions.

If the co-ordinator is not sufficiently trained to understand this and other fantasies, then she might be carried away by idealism and actually attempt to exercise omnipotence, to which I have been making reference.

Now, as the majority of group theories of which we have knowledge are derived from the experiences in therapy groups, it is also very common for a co-ordinator to indulge in the easy procedure of interpreting any recognisable process without taking into account the absence of a setting or the inopportuneness of interpreting out of context. We must bear in mind that theorisations on group mechanisms stem from two trends: the one that considers the group a unit, and the one that perceives it as an assemblage of individuals.

At this point, I shall not enter into any discussion regarding the advantages and disadvantages, mistakes or right concepts, critiques, or endorsements of these trends. I think we must focus on the opportunity to elaborate some psychic productions that are generated in work groups based on modalities that differ from those of the therapy group.

With regard to the elaborative aim that constitutes the leader's compass, I think it is impossible for him to consider the group a unity, due to the differences that exist in terms of training, qualities, competences, knowledge, and the specific functions of the participants.

In order to situate himself in that context, the leader must establish a connection between all those variables to be able to carry out his work, which will include several areas:

- understanding of the group phenomena that arise during the meetings;
- studies of resistance to progress;
- safeguarding the fulfilment of the group's aims;
- creation of a work environment;
- intervention to clarify any confusion that might arise;
- summarising the main ideas originating in the group.

These six areas demand training in group processes and sufficient experience to detect the group's fantasies, resistance to change, pathological repetitions, and evolutionary difficulties.

Even if the leader has an adequate training, her task cannot be carried out in the absence of some very precise conditions:

Conditions

Unlike in therapy groups, leaders do not have a setting, so they must create a specific setting, taking into account all the previously mentioned constants. The setting in which the productions of the group will be generated is one of the essential elements for the working-through. Co-ordinators should bear in mind what they can work with in each precise setting. It might involve a single meeting, or several meetings, of pre-established groups, of short duration groups, or be long-term projects. The group must be warned that the elaboration of the setting will include discussion and working out of the problems that facilitate group regressions, which participate in pathological repetitions, and in psychic immobility.

The team must know beforehand that the functions of the leader are only those associated with working through in order to avoid all kinds of fantasies, as, for example, the leader's wish to exercise power by maintaining regressions and the wish to control in order to perpetuate resistance to change.

There is, therefore, a previous phase aimed at clarifying all the purposes, establishing guidelines for the work, the setting, and, above all, to avoid misunderstandings.

Aims

Preparation consists of enunciating the leader's aims (let us recall that the leader must have renounced the exercise of power, which always implies a wish to maintain the participants in a regressive state) and the reasons for convening the meetings, providing a precise account of the means at her disposal, the working conditions she proposes, and the aims she pursues.

As we may see, these premises are not the same as those of therapy groups, where the proposal is to invite the participants to engage in free association. I have often observed that when leaders do not realise this difference, they convene the work team as if they were to join a therapy group, and then they are surprised at the anxieties that emerge in the meetings.

The work group needs specifications because its aim is not a therapeutic one. It is usually in this preparation phase, and in spite of all the specifications provided, that most of the fantasies involving professional differences, the leader's assessment of each participant, in addition to all the other group fantasies, emerge; it is for these reasons that the leader *must speak and not only listen*, since she must transmit "the rules of the game", that is, that all the members of the group can understand the value of their conscious and unconscious participation in the generation of common fantasies, the differences the work demands, the need to define certain functions, the chance to respect the differences, etc.

The work programmes discussed in the group might gradually replace the regressive–disorganising wishes. Research activity occupies the space where the projected fantasies were formerly generated, and the regressive group may become a work group.

The investigative attitude of the leader, who has relinquished certain regressive pleasures in order to work, study, and understand the sense of institutional activity, constitute an important stimulus that we might call motivation.

Following preparation, once the conditions of the setting have been established (times of meetings, periodicity, etc.), the working modalities must also be specified in accordance with the modality of the group: if it is a small group or a large one, a short or long duration group, inserted within a research context, or a once only meeting, as in the case of a congress, etc.

Fanaticism phenomena in psychoanalytic institutions

Although numerous groupings may exist within psychoanalytic institutions, this does not always imply contemplating the need to work in a group, not to mention the need to have specific knowledge of group functioning, its theorisations and the possibility of working through.

In general, the programmes of training institutes do not contemplate this overall perspective. It is inconceivable that psychoanalysts concerned with group elaboration should not have a favourable reception among their colleagues, as if the possibility of elaborating the psychic processes generated in the groups might be considered threatening or uncomfortable, not to say persecutory.

There might be various reasons for this. We psychoanalysts have become used to working in the framework of a relationship involving two persons, and the institution is consciously conceived as a meeting place, or a place for exchanging analytic experiences, for finding support from colleagues for this difficult practice, and, why not, as a space where our animistic and regressive tendencies are challenged, translated through a place where we seek a certain pleasure, where we seek to be understood and listened to, a place where personal narcissism may be recognised. As we shall see in the next book, the issue of narcissism is essential.

Unconsciously, everything that happens is much more varied and full of difficulties. In those organisations we may witness all the drifts described in group functioning, from the most evolved to the most primitive.

Let us take the example of a meeting convened for a lecture. The majority will attend with enthusiasm aroused by the subject matter, and, depending on the style of each psychoanalytic society, rival movements will soon appear, apparently focused on the theories employed but having—deep down—a more sinister motive that is generally narcissistic, particularly taking into account that in psychoanalytic societies, the common denominator is inbreeding. Discussions take place in this atmosphere of rivalry, of attempts to create followers, of perpetuating that inbreeding, of creating support groups, and seeking idealisation and admirers.

All these reactions and more would not constitute a problem *per se*, since they result from every encounter among humans. However, we can generalise and say that many attendees have returned to their homes in a state of anxiety and in a bad mood. What has happened? Some wonder, but others experience these feelings without even being able to name them. And meeting after meeting, a particular atmosphere that defines the institutional tone is gradually created. Few realise that, as a result of either activity or passivity, they are creating an environment that evolves towards increasingly indiscriminate and regressive institutional stances where only some ways of thinking are allowed, subtly excluding others that might turn out to be enriching. These institutional movements are slower or less indiscriminate when there are psychoanalysts who, because of their interest in group dynamics, can contribute knowledge that hinders regression and animistic thinking.

Only through an institutional analysis might the risk factors be detected and the evolution towards more primitive and archaic stances be understood. However, we can study those phenomena on the basis of direct observation, especially those that interest us the most in this case, which are the drifts towards fanaticism.

The beginning of fanaticism

Let us suppose that in a psychoanalytic society where these increasingly regressive atmospheres have been gradually created, there emerges a colleague who has formerly participated in its activities only to assert himself and create the image of a leader.

Let us suppose that many members of that society feel the need to be guided; then, obviously, the phenomenon of idealisation necessary for the consequent movement towards fanaticism will take place. This will be particularly so if the background of the leader has included a feeling of inferiority and a need to be valued (as I described earlier as part of the characteristics of the fanatic). Let us assume, in addition, that this leader is an authoritarian, passionate person with an excessive enthusiasm for a cause (let us suppose that his cause is creating groups called research groups), who believes he knows it all because he is the owner of the truth, who has Manichaean tendencies, who fights against differences, who likes to dominate and subjugate others, and, above all, who loves power.

Although I have described what at first sight can be recognised as a fanatical leader, his ways of acting, his conscious and unconscious strategies, might be very interesting, especially because very few people identify him with a fanatic. And this is particularly true if his "subjects" are ill-defined, unclear personalities, who share the thirst for power, thinking that if they participate in activities with this fantastic leader, some day they, too, will be able to be like him.

One of the strategies is that of eliminating personalities who might compete, devaluing them or criticising what they do, since, if their personalities are more mature, they are not easy to manipulate. This is the strategy of discouragement and wearing down.

The other strategy consists of forging alliances with the more fragile; in general, this is done via promises of promotions and appointments that they would never obtain if it were not for such an extraordinary "chief". To all this we might add that when this leader meets with his group of followers, he wishes to create a common language, eliminating the accursed languages, common activities to establish a group identity, in such a way that the mechanism of that group would be the idealisation of the group, which affords intense feelings of well-being and happiness.

Up to this point, nobody has been able to detect the fanatic aspect of this group, since it can be observed from the outside as an exemplary group, despite the reductionist aspect of its proposals. And since it is a question of psychoanalytic research, what is gradually created is a new perspective that will contain the seeds of intolerance, of thirst for power, and of omnipotence, aspects which are radically opposed to freedom of thought.

Let us assume that in this way psychoanalytic research might be proposed which modifies the setting, evenly floating attention, free association, interpretations, and transference, and that this new psychoanalysis propounded by the fanatical group is transformed into therapies that I shall call fanatical, *because their essential aim is to create clones*. Would this panorama not be terrifying?

Numerous authors have described the pathological strategies and alliances in the relationships among psychoanalysts. The list would be enormous, so I will highlight only the interesting work of Perdigao (2007).

Fanatical organisations

Let us recall the common denominators that may be found in fanatical organisations.

- *Overwhelming passion*, which induces us to think of an excess that appears in the form of *going beyond the limits*.
- *Violence*, so typical of sadistic drives.
- *Excessive enthusiasm* for a cause in relation to idealisations.
- *Support* for that cause and the organisation of symbiotic relationships.
- *Struggle against the sense of freedom*, difficulty in attaining maturity, feelings of inferiority.
- *Possession of the truth*, a belief that is closer to paranoid thinking than to neurosis; absence of a critical spirit and crystallisation of thought.
- *Authoritarianism, hatred of differences, Manichaeism, and dogmatism.*

However, it would not be possible for fanatical organisations to become structured and evolve without the guidance of a leader that supports and nourishes them.

In order to become thoroughly aware of the difference that might exist between a fanatical group and an evolutionary group, we must turn to the experience that examples such as those of Calvin and Savonarola have left us and ask ourselves once again why they were so successful in dragging the masses with them, even in the commission of serious crimes.

Some people might argue that those examples cannot be valid as a basis for reflection on fanaticism in psychoanalytic institutions because there it does not involve political actions or criminal behaviour. It is true that we can only resort to analogies: would destroying psychoanalysis not constitute a crime? Is politics not practised in psychoanalytical institutions?

We may distinguish a common denominator: the leaders Calvin and Savonarola had a fixed and immovable idea, an unappealable, iron conviction against freedom of thought.

In certain psychoanalytic groups, such as the imaginary examples to which I have referred, appearances are completely the opposite: the participants are invited to express themselves freely. Let us assume that the group gathers together to "think jointly" about a clinical case. All the members are free to intervene, to say whatever comes to their minds through free association, but let us suppose that, during the meeting, the leader does not compile the ideas that have been expressed with the aim of endowing them with a meaning, or interconnect them in a theoretical body of work that would help the understanding of the complexity of the problem, because what the leader is concerned with is the group discharge, a sort of abreaction that maintains idealisation: silence, in this case, generates the idealisation that we dwelt on in the chapter devoted to "Group psychology".

But if, in those groups, the leader, that is, the person who created and promoted those groups, is absent, then it is rather a question of a deification, a Supreme Ideal which, although absent, controls everything, as is attributed to God.

That leader will tend to create more and more groups, in order that supporters multiply. If to this we add that the leader in question, as in the case of Calvin, works tirelessly, in an orderly and puritanical way, that he displays apparently irreproachable behaviour, that he follows his own precepts with more dedication than anyone else, and so on, then we might think that he presents himself as a model that everyone would want to imitate.

It was said of Calvin that his great shrewdness consisted of perceiving the fragility of some people and that he utilised it thoroughly and deliberately. But it is one thing to attract followers and it is quite a different one to maintain the state of fanaticism: every example indicates that.

The great strategy is the previously mentioned veiled threat: *"Either you are with me or you are against me."*

To subject any individual to such a categorical dilemma, analogous to the one posed by the Oracle, constitutes in itself an act of violence; repeated violence constitutes a threat, and the intensity of the threat, a state of terror.

How can we conceive that this leader, who is at the same time charismatic and feared, might institute a state of terror in a psychoanalytic society? Here, we must advance in the understanding of the acquisition of power, of its exercise and maintenance, and also of the distortion of values. The exercise of power is apparently more valuable than scientific research. Furthermore, *scientific research may be utilised to exercise power.*

In certain religious examples, this utilisation of values is very evident: one may kill in God's name and commit any felony in His name.

In other works I posited the belief that there exist two general forms of power: the power to transmit and the power to dominate. I base this belief on the notion that any person has a certain amount of power over another, a power generated by the differences and by the desire for self-improvement typical of any evolution towards maturity.

Let us consider the question of knowledge. If a person has greater knowledge than another, one would expect the former to pass this knowledge on so that the latter can incorporate it. This is what I call power to transmit. But let us assume that the person who is in possession of power does not wish to transmit, because transmitting would be tantamount to accepting that the other matches up to her, or would be on a par with her regarding this knowledge, and thus would become an interlocutor instead of being reduced to submission.

Fanatics do not wish to transmit in any way, although they might present themselves as if they do and appear to be great teachers. Their

hidden intention is to dominate. They will use their power to dominate others and keep them submissive to their will. In fact, fanatics are
interested in maintaining individuals in a regressive state, in order to
fuel their dependence.

Sometimes, this intense desire to dominate others might acquire
delirious characteristics so full of conviction that reasonable arguments cannot affect them. Although fanaticism also has delirious tendencies, we cannot say that all fanatics are delirious.

Trying to discriminate between when power is aimed at transmitting and when at dominating is one of the things that is most difficult
to discern and sometimes, only the passage of time allows us to make
that differentiation.

How many times, over the course of history, have we been able to
confirm that at the moment when violent deeds occur, citizens did not
realise the magnitude of the terror, and only with the passage of time
has it been possible to judge some dictators.

Driven by those impulses to master, fanatics do not only appear
inflexible and intolerant, but they also lose respect for others, and, as
they consider them objects that can be manipulated, they do not take
their dignity into account.

CHAPTER FOUR

Respect and dignity in psychoanalysis[7]

Respect is the recognition of the fact that someone or something has worth. It can be defined as the basis of the moral grounds of ethics and morality.

Respect for interpersonal relationships begins with the individual, in the acknowledgement of the individual as a unique entity who needs the other to be understood.

The expression "human dignity" refers to the essential and non-transferable value of every human being, irrespective of social condition, race, religion, age, sex, and so on. Human dignity constitutes the basis of all rights.

For this reason, the ethical foundations of the concepts of respect and dignity do not seem to require too much explanation: respect, which can be understood as the consequence of a psychic maturing process and which translates into attitudes of consideration to others, tolerance, waiting capacity, composure, and valuation, becomes integrated in that assemblage of principles and moral rules that regulate human behaviour and relationships, as ethics is defined. The concept of dignity also includes this two-way quality: it exists in and for people. Defined as a virtue, self-esteem, deference, honesty, respectfulness, and decorum, it is also situated at the basis of ethics.

The difficulties lie in the understanding of the complex problems comprising the progressive degradation of the maintenance of respect, of the loss of the sense of dignity and even of its total abolition, a degradation that we might define as losses of the capacity to elaborate and maintain an evolutionary mental functioning, that is, in the fanatical phenomena, regressive towards the primitive mechanism of omnipotence and all that has been previously developed in animist thinking.

As I have described in other works on psychoanalytical identity, the maintenance of the analytic capacity is the result of a constant work of elaboration, a stand that opposes the idea that one can be a psychoanalyst once and for all, and that the acquisition of a certain solid and permanent maturity is a life-long event.

Then, we can ask ourselves, what is it that happens in psychoanalytic institutions which leads to regressive and de-structuring phenomena, such as fanaticism, seriously compromising the aims attributed to those institutions: to maintain, develop, and promote both the theoretical and the practical principles of the psychoanalytical foundations.

Nowadays, to refer to respect and dignity in the context of other, much more important, problems that psychoanalytical institutions have to deal with might seem somewhat trivial; however, I believe that it is important to detect the beginnings (even when they might be minimal and apparently irrelevant) of the progressive degradation of psychoanalytical ethics, from the indices that are furthest away from catastrophic situations (complete loss of the psychoanalytic foundations) to those that do not need much thought in order to be recognised.

For many psychoanalysts, maintaining and developing the analytic capacities depends exclusively on each person, a proposition that would imply a strictly individual position, as if the psychoanalyst had responsibilities towards his own self (an attitude that we could term narcissistic), denying the group and institutional responsibilities, of which very little is said, probably because their study presents difficulties that extend beyond the dual relationship (patient–analyst), a relationship that seems to constitute the only axis of reflection of any problem brought up by the psychoanalyst.

Having developed in other writings some thoughts on the psychoanalytic identity and its difficulties, I propose considering *respect and dignity as bases for the development of psychoanalytic identity*, always in constant evolution.

In these reflections, I intend to expand these two notions and consider them as guiding principles for the comprehension of some phenomena that forecast the situations that cause psychoanalysis to enter into a crisis (the crises of psychoanalysis) and lose not only its credibility but also its therapeutic efficacy.

The number of parameters that contribute to some degradation of the analytic capacities is very high (from the very pronounced pathologies to minor problems), so that, in this study, I shall restrict myself to those that seem to me to be situated at the basis of some alterations.

As I have previously described, certain dynamics created in the groups provoke regression of various kinds, as well as associated processes in which the desires of omnipotence and exercise of power prevail, parameters that acquire a great intensity in the institutional structures, to such an extent that they can cast a shadow over, and abolish, the scientific aims.

In these reflections, I would like to advance the hypothesis that the intensity of the regressive processes to animistic thinking and omnipotence can organise such a powerful form of psychic functioning that the individual who feels subjected to it, however mature he might be, might be precipitated into a regressive escalation driving him to disavowal. I would term this movement of extraordinary power a fanatical cascade, to indicate that the psychic processes plunge into an unfathomable abyss.

The effects of these processes do not seem to have been sufficiently studied: the psyche, disturbed by a functioning that exceeds it, tries to seek ways that offer an alternative to the Reality Principle and then either splits, or creates what Winnicott (1965b) termed a "false self".

In any case, the individual who suffers a fanatical cascade might appear to be a balanced person, adapted to her environment, and only some trace of the psyche (emerging processes of a primitive functioning) might indicate the precarious status of that psychic functioning.

In an attempt to put these phenomena in perspective, an example, as always imaginary, comes to my mind.

The meeting

This is about a person who, in order to have access to a certain position of power, has had to fight a great deal, using methods that have not always been very honourable: trying to gain supporters with promises of appointments, putting pressure on other colleagues by means of veiled threats, victimising himself for not having been selected at previous opportunities, raising criteria that seem convincing, distorting the concepts of scientific research, using a degree of emotional seduction (for example: "You interest me very much"), highlighting the supposed frailty of his opponents, even creating rumours aimed at devaluing other candidates, etc.

No one suspects the fanatical nature of this person because, in his fight for power, he portrays himself as humble and willing to hear other opinions, claiming that he has doubts about his own ideas and that it is his wish to help develop the psychoanalytic science.

When he has obtained his appointment, which involves acting as the leader of a group of psychoanalytic societies, in the first meeting he conscientiously prepares the subjects that must be dealt with, as is proper under such circumstances. He learns the participants' names because it is well known that when any person feels that he or she is being addressed by someone in authority who uses his or her name, there is an immediate effect of adhesion. "He considers me", *ergo*, "he respects me", a prelude to "he loves me".

The proposed programme is packed with themes that the participants are unable to understand, so that they feel ridiculous and useless. The leader announces them quickly and without any explanation and suddenly decides that one of the issues should be voted on. To this end, he gives the floor to whomever wishes to make an intervention.

Up to this point, we do not know if the leader has knowledge of the management of group processes, but we can suspect that he has intuitions based on previous observations during which he has had similar feelings while acting only as one of the participants. He knows that, under these circumstances, the group is under great tension, with members wishing to participate, speak, say something to avoid feeling considered part of a mass. For this reason, he senses that if he asks for the group's opinion, the more anxious ones will immediately speak up and say anything in an attempt to be considered with respect and, therefore, he will listen patiently, like an understanding father.

What they say does not matter, the more they rave the better; the important thing is that he is not questioned and that the issue that he has submitted to a vote is adopted. Thus, for an external observer, a kind of dialogue of the deaf takes place: some participants become aware of the group drift and remain silent because they feel that, under these circumstances, asking for precision will not be accepted. Those who intervene to voice their opinions about some subjects are approved by the leader, who indicates that he is happy with their reflections.

The group rapidly splits into two factions: those who begin to feel like supporters and those who feel like opponents, that is, not considered or loved, mostly because when they ask for the floor, it is not given to them, under the pretence that others had requested it before.

There is an atmosphere of division and confusion because the agenda has been altered; now they are talking about any subject and once again there is a proposal for voting in the next proposals: who is against?

Since many, not to say all, do not know what they are voting on, when some do not raise their hands (those who were already beginning to become supporters), the rest feel like traitors if they do not follow suit, and if they ask what it is they are voting on. And the leader quickly repeats: who is against? There is great confusion; members of both sides look at each other questioningly; nobody raises their hand. Who abstains? Then the vote is in favour of the proposal.

What is really interesting is that a part of the group feels that the meeting has been very productive while another part starts to feel depressed for not having been able to react.

This example demonstrates an obvious group manipulation, with all the features of fanaticism.

If we contemplate the example in more detail, we will be able to appreciate that the leader's group management has one primary aim: it is not about constituting an elaborative group, but about the members voting in favour of the proposals. With this intention, respect for the rest is not necessary; it would even be counterproductive, as would be consideration of their dignity, since the individuals are not seen as independent beings with freedom of expression, but, rather, as objects that can be manipulated. But there is more: the leader's manoeuvres tend to confuse, to distort the aims of the group, to hide the intention, to use the emotions, make use of omnipotence, create supporters, and so on.

If the individuals are considered partial objects, so are the ideas, the principles, the ethics, the foundations, the criteria, the bases on which knowledge, scientific theories, and their support are grounded. In short, both psychoanalytic theory and the technique are thrown into the service of other aims that are not their own. Maintaining, developing, and promoting psychoanalysis can turn into a structure based on fanaticism: to maintain the regressive status, develop omnipotence, promote supporters to create a dictatorial unit whose model is political. Thus, in a subtle way, scientific knowledge is transformed into a tool of political manipulation.

Politicisation of psychoanalysis

Politics, from the Greek πολιτικοσ (*politikós*, "citizen", "civil", "related to city planning"), is the human activity that tends to govern or direct the action of the state for the benefit of society. It is the process ideologically orientated towards decision making for the achievement of the aims of social groups. The term was widely utilised in Athens from the fifth century AD, especially thanks Aristotle's work, *Politics*. Communication endowed with power, a relationship of forces, is also defined as politics.

This subject will require more comprehensive development, and, since the matters arising from group and institutional phenomena are vast, I shall focus my analysis on what I have called the politicisation of psychoanalysis, the effects of which organise systems of pathological relationships that undermine the bases of psychoanalysis and distort it.

This concept (politicisation) can lead to confusion. If we understand politics as an internal attitude towards certain events linked to a country's governance and even an institutional position in the face of social problems which can alter the scientific qualities, then we can infer that all human beings are political.

In these brief reflections, I shall not refer to these matters but to the study of some group and institutional problems inserted in the unconscious relational networks that bear the marks of idealisations of power and dominance, so opposed to respect and dignity.

We might find the roots of the politicisation of psychoanalysis, a phenomenon which is not hard to understand but whose consequences I believe have not been sufficiently studied, in the history of psychoanalysis.

To understand these consequences, I shall reflect on three subjects that seem essential to me: the consequences of the politicisation of psychoanalysis, the symbiotic community, and identification with the aggressor.

Consequences of the politicisation of psychoanalysis

Psychoanalytical institutions are characterised by a community of individuals that is close to what we might call inbreeding, which I deal with elsewhere, and which creates specific interactions in their groups in addition to the group dynamics typical of any other human group. However, the creation and stability of these institutions is a function of a series of aims defined by the maintenance, the development and the diffusion of psychoanalysis.

Probably, the political model was also used to manage the institutional activities: a government with its president and an assemblage of persons who constitute the Board of Directors or The Executive, as well as a series of groups in charge of organising specific activities (institute of psychoanalysis, centres for general medical attention, publications, etc.). The assemblage is governed by a system of assemblies equivalent in politics to a meeting of leaders to whom the citizens have delegated their ambitions.

This model does not seem to have been questioned globally in terms of its situational inadequacy (the situation of a country is not the same as that of a scientific institution), of its means (the laws of a government to guarantee the co-operation of individuals who might evince great differences: economical, professional, social, ideological, etc.), and, above all, of its conditions and aims.

The means (psychoanalytical knowledge), the conditions of maintenance of the psychoanalytical specificity (organisation of congresses, scientific activities, and the identification phenomena created in these situations), and the institutional aims cannot be compared to the situations created in a country.

However, if we wish to understand the persistence of inadequate structures (inadequacy among conditions, means, and aims), we must question the secondary benefits that are produced and the amount of fantasies that feed them.

One of the subjects would be the problem of the satisfaction–dissatisfaction of the psychoanalytical practice. If the analytical experience is accompanied by a sufficiently gratifying motivation, one would not need to project on to the groups and institutions the frustration resulting from an excessive idealisation, idealisation that turns a scientific institution into a country, its organisation into a state, its procedures into hierarchies of values, and so on. The frayed edges of omnipotence are widely reflected.

Another issue is the problem of narcissistic personalities of an extreme frailty who seek pathological alliances (pathological because they are governed by implicit threats, perverse promises, fetishism, and manipulations) in the institutional groups, creating tensions because of the incessant struggles for the exercise of power and dominance. Due to the destructive forces they employ, these personalities are considered models of omnipotence, inducing identifications with the aggressor whose consequences can be harmful to psychoanalytical identity, which, for these personalities, is based on quasi-religious conceptions, on dogmatic types of training that do not allow criticism from the outside (from which nothing is expected, since self-sufficiency is absolute).

Institutional politicisation is, thus, the loss of criteria that govern scientific activities and their substitution for regressive values of animistic thinking (associated to power, omnipotence, submission, robotisation, etc., values conceived as political needs to govern the institution) inserted in the trajectory of the principle of pleasure where the principle of reality is disavowed.

Scientific activities (congresses, lectures, symposia, etc.) organised in these situations carry the seal of narcissistic valuations, the institutional activities of promotion of members to full members or training analysts are at the service of pathological alliances, and the psychoanalytical quality is subjected to theoretical domination (psychoanalytical schools that in certain situations are considered noble, while in others they are undervalued or idealised).

Such domination and omnipotence are opposed to respect and dignity, whose indices of degradation allow us to understand the progressive loss of the psychoanalytical identity and make us forget that respect and dignity are based on individual achievement, a relational practice, and institutional ethics.

Politicisation of psychoanalysis, the roots of which are found in the regression to animistic thinking, has the aim of maintaining and developing the regressive states in group experiences and in the institutional exchanges, either by denying the importance of group identification or simply by turning the institution into an object that can be manipulated, positions whose defence is often based on a confusion between individual and group.

For this reason, I believe it is important to try to understand the differences between individual psychology and group psychology, in order to avoid viewing the individual as a victim of the group and the group as a simple assemblage of individuals.

In short, politicisation of psychoanalysis is inserted in the regressive trajectory in which the values of respect and dignity are replaced by omnipotence. The exercise of power and the tendency to domination are presented as psychoanalytical ideals and replace the scientific competences that demand humility and the capacity to mourn and to elaborate. In this way, the maintenance of psychoanalysis becomes transformed into the maintenance of omnipotence, and the development of psychoanalysis into identification with the aggressor. What is worse, if politicisation is often a conscious procedure, tendencies leading to symbiosis and identification with the aggressor are unconscious, lending themselves to multiple psychic manoeuvres which are very difficult to recognise and even more difficult to elaborate.

To better understand the degradation of psychoanalytical identity to politicisation, it is necessary to reflect on the confusional processes employed when justifying the need of a government to organise the tasks of an institution.

Although it is true that scientific activities require a certain organisation, such an organisation cannot be governed by the same parameters as the government of a nation. In psychoanalytical institutions, the assemblies formed by the members are the ones that elect the directors of the organisations.

In politicisation, and under the premise of unconscious omnipotence, the directors represent the noble class that must keep order and preserve the security of its members. Thus, open or veiled struggles to recover dominance are often started, sometimes by the assembly, and sometimes by the directing body.

The concepts of democracy, executive power, sovereignty, etc., are employed to convince the adversary, and the arguments used according to the shrewdness of each faction are placed at the service of the power struggle in which psychoanalysis as a science and as a practice is relegated to theoretical–abusive counter-argumentations.

In these situations, which often exceed both the directors and the members because of their unconscious features, many reactions can occur: for example, attempts at unification to neutralise highly dangerous splits or fuelling of group divisions.

The attempts at unification can evolve through primitive mechanisms: setting up of sacrificial rituals, transformed into paradoxical proceedings for the acquisition of institutional categories, through symbiotic mechanisms, or by increasingly complex and hierarchical pyramidal structures, which generate identification with the aggressor.

Generally, these three forms alternate according to the circumstances and the regressive status of the groups. But they all carry the seal of the symbiotic constellations.

The symbiotic community

The symbiotic community is governed by the confusional postulate which states that all the members of a same family should be equal, think alike, feel the same way, and be perfectly transparent, united, and inseparable.

Expressions such as, "In the institution there is room for all", "We have to be united", "The institution protects", and so on, indicate an idealisation of the institutional structures through which the efforts to procure peace and welfare for all, as well as the abolition of any conflict, are highlighted.

In these situations, the scientific co-ordination is transformed into a monarchy, creating pathological relational networks, since the hierarchy represents a divinised being on whom all the ideals are projected and who occupies the individuals' egos, so that they feel relegated to simple objects, but, at the same time, happy to share the common fantasy of omnipotence.

The mechanisms that such situations might generate often become increasingly complex: from disavowal of reality to the symbiotic relational dilemma (the fusion provides a feeling of completeness but, at the same time, a sensation of loss of the person's own personality), the defence mechanisms utilised (absence of differences, destructive alliances, splitting into clans, exclusion or elimination of the most differentiated, and, at other moments, grandiose offers to share power, etc.), all have a common aim: to maintain confusion so as to guarantee domination.

Symbiotic institutional functioning is characterised by the concealment of information, manipulation, decision making in semi-clandestine meetings, the nurturing of fantasies due to lack of precision, aggressive strategies (raising the voice excessively to intimidate, insult, or utter contemptuous reflections, etc.), controlling management, and, above all, the idealisation of the hierarchy.

We may regard the persons who represent this type of functioning or share the attitudes of omnipotence as aggressors, since those who advocate the symbiotic community annul the other's personality.

Identification with the aggressor

Just as in the symbiotic unit, the processes that develop in an almost totally unconscious way leave the drive derivatives exposed, and utilise defences of a primitive or archaic nature. As its name indicates, and as shown in the numerous works developed by the American School, this identification implies an introjection by the aggressor and a projection of the aggression to the external world.

The result of this identification is not an evolutionary change of the ego, but a submission to the aggressor's will and a feeling of intense love for him.

Identification with the aggressor constitutes, in this sense, a basic proof of symbiotic unity and, due to its sadistic–masochistic components, an extraordinary reinforcement of the pathological affective bonds, where respect and dignity disappear as relational values.

The ego ideal, in this case, is constituted by regressive aspects of contempt, disqualification, paradoxical messages, and so on, which convey to these groups an aspect of a primitive system which, seen from the outside, produces fear and rejection.

Identification with the aggressor inserted in the symbiotic unity is, in reality, a *dictatorship masquerading as democracy*. It is a dictatorship because only a few decide, think, organise, speak, establish, distribute, and argue for the rest. It is democratic in appearance because, having asked for the group's approval or consensus on subjects treated beforehand and decided in advance, the matter is really to impose the decision that has already been made, as we could see in the example presented above.

Identification with the aggressor can cause serious damage in a group, since all those who operate on the basis of this identification behave as the leaders, and are sometimes more cruel than the actual leaders, producing a great many splits, numerous struggles for small portions of power, considering any task magnified by the leaders an achievement of the ideal.

Institutional structures under the yoke of identification with the aggressor, if they are hierarchical (members of different categories), often serve the exercise of domination by a number of individuals, who request the other categories to do what they are not capable of doing, saying, or thinking themselves.

Due to its anal characteristics, identification with the aggressor accompanies unconscious fantasies of a homosexual, perverse, aggressive nature, expulsive or retentive, obsessive and conservative, that in the institutional relationships acquire very characteristic forms: to take advantage of the other by any means, attacking him by surprise, convincing him of his masochist needs (the more the other suffers, the more he will benefit, etc.), expressing great affection only to hurt him later, etc.

Identification with the aggressor constitutes the complete opposite of respect and dignity, concepts which are not recognised and which are mentioned only to despise them or denigrate them.

So far, I have attempted to analyse thoroughly and sometimes specify the constellations that surround fanaticism, the range of their characteristics, and the breadth of their expressions; fanatical mechanisms, the ways in which they develop and their consequences, which depend on their intensity, sometimes discreet and sometimes dramatic, not to say terrifying, the processes on which they feed and try to perpetuate, and the effects that they can have on psychoanalytical science as a whole. However, we might wonder: would all this knowledge enable us to fight against such a devitalising plague?

CHAPTER FIVE

Can fanaticism be combated?

In the opinion of the Egyptian writer, Alaa Al Aswany, "If you understand art you will never be a fanatic and if you are a fanatic, keep yourself away from art because you will never understand it" (Al Aswany, 2012). For this reason, he adds that the majority of the few fanatics who had attacked me had not read his novel. In his most recent novel, *Chicago* (2008), he has stated that religious fanaticism and literature are incompatible.

Oz (2012)[2006] explains that, in his view,

> the essence of fanaticism lies in the desire to force other people to change . . . One way or another, the fanatic is more interested in you than in himself, for the very simple reason that the fanatic has a very little self or no self at all. (2012, pp. 65–66)

And he gives us his opinion regarding the way to cure fanaticism. How can we cure ourselves of fanaticism? Imagination, literature, and humour is the recipe proposed by this author as effective antidotes against fanaticism, since literature and imagination might help us to visualise, through fiction, the ravages caused by fanaticism, although there is much literary material that has fuelled hatred and feelings of superiority. Humour would contribute to overcoming fanaticism, since fanatics take themselves so seriously that they are incapable of laughing at themselves.

> I have never once in my life seen a fanatic with a sense of humour, nor have I ever seen a person with a sense of humour becoming a fanatic, unless he or she has lost that sense of humour. Fanatics are often sarcastic. Some of them have a very pointed sense of sarcasm, but no humour. Humour contains the ability to laugh at ourselves. (Oz, 2012, pp. 71–72)

However, and although I share the stance of these writers, we cannot consider the possibility that people imbued with fanaticism might change simply as a result of being told to read or to have a sense of humour.

The processes of personality change, upon which I have expounded elsewhere (Utrilla Robles, 2010) are the result of arduous and difficult psychic work that we term elaborations and that psychoanalysis helps us to carry out. Nevertheless, we have to raise the issue in a different way, since the fanaticism to which I am making reference is the one with which certain psychoanalysts are imbued. What has happened? Has psychoanalysis not helped them to change?

It would, therefore, not be a question of changing fanatics, but of not adhering to their causes, not supporting them, detecting them and hindering their strategies, not becoming their followers, not admiring them, and a whole series of other oppositional "no's". We might ask ourselves: what nourishes these fanatics who continue to exist in psychoanalytic institutions? Let us analyse this in more detail. In all the preceding examples, beginning with the film *The Wave* and continuing with Castellio's experience, we may notice that the fight against fanaticism is very difficult because it would require an opposing force of equal intensity and characteristics. Francisco Goya's painting, *The Colossus* (ca 1808–1812), offers us a metaphorical example of a fight to the death that only two fanatics could engage in.

In Castellio's case, the stances are different because this brave opponent of Calvin used highly scientific arguments, since he was the possessor of vast and deep knowledge on philosophical and theological issues, and his aspirations were related exclusively to the quest for truth. But what Stefan Zweig demonstrates is that violence cannot be defeated with arguments from conscience.

Unfortunately, this has proved to be a recurring experience in the case of destructive dictatorships over the course of history. It is true that the historical experience teaches us that if no changes are produced in the consciences of those who experience the fanatical events, over the course of time these experiences can apparently leave a memory that, little by little, would produce changes in the mentality of human beings and the wish to combat those fanaticisms. We can put forward the idea that in the immediate term, the fight against fanaticism is possible, but not so its defeat, for which reason it is always worthwhile trying to detect, understand, elaborate, and overcome those phenomena that are so disturbing and devastating.

Let us begin by questioning ourselves: are there any situations that may provoke in each of us the regressions I have described? Are there any situations that propitiate fanaticism?

If we bear in mind that fanaticism is a "short route" mental functioning, as Chasseguet-Smirgel (1990, 2001) described it, in contrast with the "long route" quality characterising any quest for knowledge, which demands humility, the capacity to become depressed, of doubting, of relinquishing regressive pleasures, of constant and sometimes arduous psychic work, then we shall understand that the personalities that do not doubt or make any effort to understand what happens to them or to those around them apparently choose an easier and more successful life, a saving of mental energy, a feeling of safety that symbiotic communities offer, the possibility of avoiding fear of failure and uncertainty, of feeling safe and strong. In short, they choose the opportunity to acquire that which everyone desires in a fast and effective way. Is not that what our current society asks from us?

Let us suppose that a person dreams of having a beautiful house and a college degree, of feeling valued by those around him, of being a hero, of having a satisfactory job and managing a company, owning a fantastic car, dominating others, and so on. Let us further suppose that all this is granted to him without the need to make any effort to study, work, save money to buy a house and a car, without having to demonstrate his skills, or make others value and love him. Who would not want to have all this and to obtain it in this way?

Not everyone, however, would be ready to use violence in order to achieve this, no matter how attractive the project might seem.

This description might represent what I call the fanatic idyll, because, in fact, fanatical personalities are also characterised by a high level of anxiety, a constant state of unrest, a permanent wasting of their time, a persistent search for supporters and followers, an effort to control others, and they probably have many conflicts to solve.

Fanaticism and its constellations

All the descriptions I have been able to gather together in order to expand on and specify what a fanatical personality, its constellations, and its impact on psychoanalytic institutions are, focus, as we have been able to confirm, on the issues of regressions, omnipotence, and animistic thinking, with a whole amalgam of spectres and dimensions associated to groups and institutions.

However, we must consider the fact that not all fanatics are the same; not all resort to the same methods and strategies, and neither do they do it with the same intensity. In the examples of Calvin and Savonarola I could appreciate certain similarities, but in the other imaginary examples of fanatic leaders in psychoanalytic institutions— less spectacular than the former—there are varieties that depend on a series of parameters which are not always well defined, but which have a common denominator: the tendency to be delimited either by narcissistic factors or by paranoid or melancholic tendencies.

In the course of my passage through institutions, I have had experiences that have given me the opportunity to develop a sort of sensibility for detecting the subtle movements to which I have made reference, and even to be able to formulate hypotheses forecasting their future.

In some experiences described in the form of examples, which I have modified so that no person would be able to recognise him or herself, I have verified that many of those fanatical leaders have failed in their attempts to perpetuate fanatical situations, becoming less idealised and even somewhat despised individuals after some years of domination. The time of glory and power has dragged them, like any other human being, towards banality and oblivion. But it is also true that this is not the case of all fanatics, for there are some who have left an indelible imprint. What leads us to think about the possible existence of different fanatical intensities, and even fanatical moments, not to say fanatical instances of diverse categories.

We may ask ourselves: what do situations of fanaticism consist of? And, also, may one hold so-called positions of power without falling into a fanatical drift?

Bearing in mind that I believe that nobody has completely renounced the omnipotent positions of childhood, and that regressive trends seem to hide in the nooks and crannies of our psyche, we must assume that in the presence of situations favouring the development of our grandiose domination expectations, we could all become beings in search of glory and vanity, for which we must forget the devitalising risks of any fanatical practice: limitation of freedom, impoverishment of the psyche, insensitivity to others, loss of respect and dignity that might turn against oneself, certain isolation, and, above all, loss of psychoanalytic skills.

Situations involving fanaticism always seem to make their appearance in the presence of idealisations; hence, these represent the indices of possibilities of fanaticism. Can we think that when we are idealised we are offered the temptation to become fanatics, especially bearing in mind that the human being needs to idealise in order to negotiate his or her paranoid tendencies?

I have not addressed in this study the similarities between fanaticism, paranoia, and melancholy, although many of the descriptions appear to overlap, and I have addressed this issue elsewhere in more depth (Utrilla Robles, 2010), for which reason at this point I will limit myself to outlining it.

The sinister one

In a psychoanalytic institution, a member who had always shown himself to be taciturn, ready to appear as a victim of any event (a victim mentality that gave him a certain prestige because all his colleagues referred to him by saying "Poor Mr X who suffers so much! What a good person he is!"), ran for a position of responsibility when he had previously criticised the existence in institutions of categories that he considered humiliating. Why are there associate members and full members, and members with a didactic function, when all these scales of value correspond, in his opinion, to positions of prestige derived from varieties of favouritism and situations of submission? His melancholic tonality aroused in many colleagues the wish to take care of him and protect him, the prelude of a certain degree of affective support which X utilised to make people love and esteem him.

In this position of responsibility, X underwent a transformation: the level of demand exerted on those beneath him increased; little by little, he announced criteria for accessing other categories which appeared to be disproportionate, as if the applicants had to prove that they were already members with didactic functions, to the extent that the applicants' tests and papers became true sacrificial exercises; he posed terrifying questions on personal aspects, questions regarding institutional functioning that might involve other members, requirements of diagnostic perfection, questionings about clinical aspects, and so on.

Many of those who "loved" him began to consider that he was strong and fantastic, that at last somebody had dared to make demands and establish order, that he was a leader capable of transforming the level of the institution, raising it and fostering a psychoanalytic quality which had not existed before; the institution needed a distinguished member to afford it value and prestige. Other colleagues, who doubted his abilities, showed themselves to be cautious and critical, but X perceived each difference of opinion as a personal insult and consequently tried to "eliminate" them through all possible strategies—disseminating rumours regarding their integrity, calling each proposal into question, detracting from their credibility, even using veiled threats of adducing lack of reasonable criteria and obstacles in order that they might never have access to positions of prestige.

Among his supporters, things were different. Everything was praise, promotions, and congratulations on the smallest proposal, and he was continuously forging alliances to convince them of the excellence of his ideas and of how he would share those ideas with them. The subliminal message was the transformation of the institution into a structure rendered unique by its value and its prestige, as well the transformation of psychoanalysis into a universal practice that would be at everyone's service and solve all problems.

He resorted to all sorts of manoeuvres in order to nurture that grandiose aspect. In the case of his detractors, he portrayed himself as a victim, to whom they caused enormous suffering, displaying an intense pain at the meetings, which produced the effect of rage and rejection in his supporters focused on those who seemed to be his enemies. Apparently, X wished to convey a message of goodness. All he did was for the benefit of psychoanalysis, which deserved everything: his time, dedication, and effort; he would even give his life for it.

For those who loved psychoanalysis, this message was encouraging, and little by little the number of his supporters increased to the point of creating an atmosphere of idealisation in which psychoanalysis and his own person overlapped. He *was* psychoanalysis.

In order to maintain this atmosphere, the procedures were repeated: the enemies transformed into persecutors must disappear, converting them to "the cause". With great cunning, he appointed them leaders of some groups after having established multiple commissions—widely controlled leaderships. Since many of those commissions were not of great use, he let them fail in order to reproach their leaders. Those former opponents lost their dignity and they no longer dared to criticise him.

But, despite these transformations (devitalised opponents, increasingly enthusiastic supporters), X appeared to be more and more persecuted, and, hence, worked tirelessly to detect the slightest sign of controversy. His melancholic aspect turned into a manic one (he had promoted so many activities that nobody could attend all of them); he was available day and night, and nothing seemed to cause him exhaustion, such was his pleasure in dominating others. (It is interesting to point out that as early as 1621, the English clergyman Robert Burton, in his *Anatomy of Melancholy*, included fanatic morbidity under the notion of "melancholy").

Might we speak of a fanatical, manic, paranoid personality, or, rather, of a fanatical, manic, paranoid situation?

In spite of these strong adjectives, which look rather like diagnostic judgements, few people in the institution appeared to be sensitive to the state in which that institution found itself. But what I deem most worrying is that X's project to create groups and commissions to better manipulate all the members strongly resonated with other institutions, always following the short-term approach that I mentioned earlier. Leaders with no knowledge of group processes were appointed, groups with no definite settings were created (the criterion applied was that the members get to know each other better), and, above all, the aims of these groups were highly fanaticised. The apparently scientific objectives concealed an extensive movement aimed at *unifying psychoanalysis* (unification of languages, theories, and practices), dispossessing it of its essence of freedom of thought. In that atmosphere, the use of a single language for all countries, a language that all psychoanalysts should know and master, was advocated.

In this rather schematic example, we might also appreciate what I called the politicisation of psychoanalysis. Psychoanalysis was actually an *object* to be utilised in X's political manoeuvres: to create power structures as if the psychoanalytic institution were a country governed by a unifier who knew what was good for others, who thought in their stead, and decided what was most convenient for them.

Although for many years I considered that group processes ought to be better known and more frequently used within psychoanalytic institutions, when I realised that group meetings could be used to achieve fanatical aims, I became discouraged and thought it necessary to denounce these practices in an attempt to think, argue, theorise, and elaborate. How can the opposite pole of fanaticism be presented with the profusion of detail I have tried to contribute in order to detect, understand, and elaborate fanatical movements?

The Odyssey

In order to provide an answer to the previous question, reference would have to be made to all the knowledge we possess on psychoanalytic practice and theory, a task which is impossible to achieve in this book, but which Freud bequeathed to us for its continuous study and consideration. For I believe that Freud's *oeuvre* is the indispensable reference in which to find models to combat fanaticism. In fact, *the opposite pole of fanaticism is psychoanalysis*.

And since I consider that, in his essay translated as *Civilization and its Discontents*[8] (1930a), Freud provides us with the clues to these elaborations, I made an interpretation that might be very personal (each of Freud's writings can be studied in very different works) and I considered it a human Odyssey.

For those of us for whom *Civilization and its Discontents* represents an odyssey comparable to that of Ulysses or *The Aeneid* in this psychic adventure in which we all participate, we cannot but be in awe at the magnitude of what we intuit in this text by Freud.

So many things have been said about Freud; he has been interpreted in so many languages (and here I refer to psychoanalytic theories); he has been envisaged from the perspective of sociology and philosophy, of empiricist sciences and literature, that it would seem almost a provocation to attempt to add something more, even if it is only a dream or a silence emanating from the thoughts of those many others. As Pablo Neruda expressed, "Let me come to be still in your silence"[9] (Neruda, 2007[1924], p. 39), which here might be transformed into, "Let me speak with your words". However, returning to the poet's words when he says, "The memory of you emerges from the night around me" (Neruda 2007[1924], p. 55), I suddenly associate some passages from Freud with other writings—that of Baricco in his most recent book, *An Iliad* (2004). This is perhaps because *The Iliad* is a song to the gods, to men and to heroes, memorable for their ire and their ambition, for their audacity and their cunning, for their revenge and their piety, within the boundaries of an eternal battlefield. And Freud, precisely, will transport us to that battlefield of drives, of repressed affects, of pleasure and displeasure, of well-being and the suffering that precedes it, in a word, of the *search for happiness*. Of course, the whole of mankind is involved in that endless quest to love and be loved, to recognise and be recognised, valued, dignified, and distinguished.

Freud does not tell us about the beginning or the end of that adventure. In another text he has warned us about this: what is important is not the beginning of a journey, or the station from whence the train departs, or the one where it arrives. What is important is the journey.

Let us travel, then, if possible, in the manner of Ulysses.

The feeling of eternity

> It is impossible to escape the impression that people commonly use false standards of measurement – that they seek power, success and wealth for themselves and admire them in others and that they underestimate what is of true value in life. (Freud, 1930a, p. 64)

This introduction to *Civilization and its Discontents* already arouses uneasiness. What is it that life offers us? How can we get to perceive, to brush, or to experience that feeling of eternity that Freud also terms "oceanic" (Freud, 1930a, p. 64)?

This phrase deserves reflection. Many Freud scholars have believed they perceived in his work a sort of solipsism, as if the creator of psychoanalysis had "entered the psychic world" in order to investigate its processes, forgetting the world around him, and when I say "world", I am referring to society, the environment, external reality, culture, etc. Let us begin with culture. The translation from German— *kultur*—does not seem to be right according to scholars; it seems that Freud meant, rather, civilisation in its wider sense. And here we start to foresee the scope of this phrase: why do people commonly use false standards? That is to say, why is Freud's *oeuvre* understood as an intrapsychic investigation, when, in fact, it only speaks of man in his environment, connected to his parents, family, ancestors, even primitive generations?

Since I will not be able to develop to their full extent two hypotheses inspired by this work by Freud, I will simply posit them and leave my exposition unfinished.

The departure station does not represent the drives, but everything that precedes them: the primitive horde, the origins of humankind, the glacial eras. The journey is constituted by those Homeric characters going on stage to narrate their story of passion and blood, their great war, their great adventure.

The second hypothesis is that this work by Freud, which many have termed "Civilization's Well-Being", is not the station at which we arrive, either—a kind of delta, the culmination of a whole body of successful psychic work. And we understand by the successful lifting of repression the elaboration of fantasies, the overcoming of the Oedipus complex, with all its corollaries of integration of the libidinal stages, the complex tissues of identification, repetition compulsion, memories, and reconstructions. And all this through the analytic relation achieved through transference neurosis, which I have called analytic neurosis elsewhere, and countertransference work.

The point is not, therefore, to become a perfect being with no conflicts or sufferings, who might organise a space of civilisation, a kind of paradise of successful men and deified heroes. The point is acquiring that elaborative ability that allows us to connect with the world and with ourselves in search of that lost Arc that is happiness.

A subjective experience

Freud invites us, from the very beginning, to reflect on the problem of boundaries, an issue I will not be able to summarise in a few words, but, as previously, I will posit another hypothesis: the more limited we may be, the better we appropriate the universe around us. This is an apparently paradoxical pronouncement, since it implies extremes, from the minimum to the maximum; it would mean that the smaller we are, the greater we can be.

In fact, the point is very simple, and it is called integration; let us call it integration of the partial drives during the anal phase, which inaugurates the object relation, or the integration of the libidinal stages in genitality, or the integration of pregenitality in the Oedipus complex. In order to integrate (that is, to think that something we perceive outside might form part of our inner world), boundaries are required. And boundaries are built using thoughts and words, which is tantamount to saying through the relationship with others.

> In this way, then, the ego detaches itself from the external world, or to put it more correctly, originally the ego includes everything, later it separates off an external world from itself. Our present ego-feeling is, therefore, only a shrunken residue of a much more inclusive – indeed, an all-embracing – feeling which corresponded to a more intimate bond between the ego and the world about it. If we may assume that there are many people in whose mental life this primary ego-feeling has persisted to a greater or lesser degree, it would exist in them side by side with the narrower and more sharply demarcated ego-feeling of maturity, like a kind of counterpart to it. In that case, the ideational contents appropriate to it would be precisely those of limitlessness and of a bond with the universe – the same ideas with which my friend elucidated the 'oceanic' feeling.

> But have we a right to assume the survival of something that was originally there, alongside of what was later derived from it? (Freud, 1930a, p. 68)

Freud continues his reflection, confronting us with the problem of illusion (starting from religious feelings), and on this subject, how can we leave Winnicott, the wizard of illusions, aside?

But for Winnicott (1971), the space of illusion is built through the early relationship with the mother, more or less in these terms: the child cries, makes a gesture, screams, moans . . . the mother interprets all these signs as demands to which she must respond. In itself, this is a delirium: to believe that the other asks for something without having expressed it, and to respond because one thinks that the other has asked for what one has imagined. It matters little.

Thanks to what is known as mother–child identification, the mother can offer the baby a series of stimuli, caresses, breastfeeding, words, and so on, through which the baby will build a series of sensations which are essential for his neurological and psychic evolution.

Combined activities, nuanced responses, impressions, sensations; all this gradually creates the so-called space of illusion.

We may imagine this space as follows: the baby cries, the mother thinks he is hungry, she breastfeeds him, the child calms down, the mother is satisfied because she was right, the child gives her pleasure. Her actions are based on assumptions . . . perhaps the child is hungry. And it turns out that she was right. At other moments, the mother might think that if she was right once, she might be right again, and this will prevent her from despairing.

This attitude of the mother of extreme sensitivity is what leads her to perceive the needs of the child, responding to them and providing him with something almost at the precise moment and in the convenient place ("place" understood in the sense of the needs associated to the child's drives; the mouth, the skin, certain parts of the body, etc.); this attitude of the mother depends, then, on a state of mind, on the way in which those around her behave towards her, on the amount of satisfaction she obtains from the baby, on her regressive possibilities, that is, her capacity to identify herself with a baby as if she herself could be a baby, be in the place of her child, and of her attitude contributing to separate herself from the child, renounce, even though it is only for a given time lapse, those amorous and satisfactory exchanges.

Why can one relinquish an activity that affords one intense pleasure? Put simply, because there is another activity in store, which will also afford, if not the same pleasure, a different but important pleasure.

However, in Freud's view, the creation of illusion is based on the infatuation that produces a blurring between the ego and the other, described by other authors (for example, see David, 1974) as a pathological state of disintegration of the personality, verging on delirium.

It is interesting to corroborate that in this essay Freud leads us along the path of normal delirium represented by a capacity to delimit oneself without falling into the abyss of psychosis. For this reason, it is understandable that he should begin by questioning himself about the religions that might also produce those illusions via beliefs verging on unreality.

Personally, I can imagine that the "oceanic feeling" might have come to relate itself subsequently with religion, for this interior-being-one-with-the-whole, implicit in its ideational content, seduces us like a first attempt at religious consolation, like another path to refute the danger that the ego recognises, threatening, in the external world.

And at this moment, Freud leads us to the eternal question: how can man retain his omnipotence without constructing a paranoid state?

The answer seems to be contained in suffering.

> It is no wonder if, under the pressure of these possibilities of suffering, men are accustomed to moderate their claims to happiness – just as the pleasure principle itself, indeed, under the influence of the external world, changed into the more modest reality principle – if a man thinks himself happy merely to have escaped unhappiness or to have survived his suffering, and if in general the task of avoiding suffering pushes that of obtaining pleasure into the background. (Freud, 1930a, p. 77)

The art of living

The multiple ruses that the human being resorts to with the aim of avoiding suffering and preserving pleasure belong to the realm of imagination (and I stress the fact that I am not saying imaginary), but maintaining the boundaries of reality that Freud calls the reality principle. And although in this essay he does not delve into the ramifications of the constitution of this reality principle, it is a fact that in our psychoanalytic experience we confirm that it is the hardest to acquire. In other works, I have called this *relational sensitivity*, indicating that the elaboration of our narcissistic tendencies allows us to become sensitive to the needs of others and respond without invading or subjugating, characteristics that imply an extreme difficulty. Because, just as Freud explains to us how we might find the external world to be threatening, we might deduce that other human beings always represent a possible threat, in such a way that our response would always be to dominate in order not to be possessed.

Happiness—considered in its narrow sense—whose achievement seems possible is merely a question of each individual's libidinal economy. No rule in this respect is valid for everyone; each person must seek the way in which he or she may be happy. Their choice of the road to follow will be influenced by the most diverse factors. It all depends on the sum of actual satisfaction they may expect from the external world and on the extent to which they tend to become independent from it; finally, also on the strength they develop to modify it according to their wishes.

You might ask: how can one acquire the longed-for happiness if it carries with it so much suffering, so many narcissistic wounds, so much renunciation? Or, in reply to the question of whether it is necessary to suffer in order to be happy, we might say that the core of the problem lies in the *community*, whether this is a group of persons or a community of affects, let us call it society on the whole, cohabiting, sharing, and exchanging. From the moment that we live in a community, mathematical rules will prevail: for instance, if I love a person, I will not tolerate being abandoned on account of another who wants to love the same person. That is an intolerable equation, and even though there is a pretence that love may be shared, the initial tendency is one of exclusiveness.

One plus one does not equal two, nor two plus one, three. Only when the pleasure of sharing is stronger than the fear of losing is the sense of beauty associated with that of freedom, as stated by François Cheng (a great writer of the French Academy who has many publications on Chinese poetry to his credit), in order to save the world—from barbarism, it is understood. This phrase, "Beauty will save the world" (Cheng, 2009[2006], p. 6), is Dostoevsky's (from *The Idiot*, first published in 1869), and Cheng further elaborates, saying that our time is characterised by the confusion of values. And I would add confusion of competences, confusion of fields of knowledge, in which differences tend to be abolished, and without differences there is no exchange: *without exchange there is no respect and without respect, there is no dignity.*

Thus, we see multiple perspectives from which to understand the art of living: elaboration on our psychic world, understanding of the wishes of others, respect and dignity, acknowledgment of differences, and exchanges.

But the task is not as easy as might be intuited. The art of living does not depend solely on the maturity of each individual.

The liberty of the individual is not a benefit of culture. It was greatest before any culture, though, indeed, it had little value at that time, because the individual was hardly in a position to defend it. Liberty has undergone restrictions throughout the evolution of civilisation, and justice demands that these restrictions shall apply to all.

It is here that Freud will raise our awareness regarding these issues; "observing" them from perspectives other than psychoanalysis, they can contribute new cultural values, ideas open to debate as long as we situate them in the place from where they emanate, so that the confusion between ethics, sociology, economy, and psychoanalysis does not contribute to marring the beauty that each position contains. One can also say that these other sciences might wonder why Freud found it necessary to resort to civilisation, translated as culture, to refer to man's happiness.

The answer came through the creation of a new psychoanalytic concept: the superego (Freud, 1920g, 1923b), and permit me the audacity of referring to the superego as a civilisation within each one of us.

This analogy between the cultural process and the individual's evolution can be taken much further, for it could be stated that the community, too, develops a superego under whose influence cultural evolution takes place. "The cultural superego has developed its ideals and set up its demands. Among the latter, those which deal with the relations of human beings to one another are comprised under the heading of ethics" (Freud, 1930a, p. 142).

However, for Freud love is not enough, and here I refer to an idea of Bettelheim, for whom the simple fact of loving does not guarantee the evolution of a therapy; "Love is not enough" (1950). Love is inevitably linked to hatred, to rage, to aggression. This is an equation that is simple to understand: when I love in an exclusive way, I hate those who can take that love away from me and I feel like attacking them. But Freud, as usual, goes one step further:

> their neighbour is for them not only a potential helper or sexual object, but also someone who tempts them to gratify their aggressiveness on him, to exploit his capacity for work without compensation, to use him

sexually without his consent, to seize his possessions, to humiliate him, to cause him pain, to torture and to kill him. (Freud, 1930a, p. 111)

The existence of this inclination to aggression, which we can detect in ourselves, and which is derived from the duality of our life and death instincts, will disturb our relations with our neighbours, says Freud, since it "forces civilization into such a high expenditure [of energy]" (1930a, p. 112).

Does the aggression and self-destruction instinct transmit itself from individual man to civilisation, Freud wonders. Or is it the force of love, of the "eternal Eros, [who] will make an effort to assert himself in the struggle with his equally immortal adversary. But who can foresee with what success and with what result? (1930a, p. 145).

Freud continues by saying, "Sublimation of instinct is an especially conspicuous feature of cultural evolution; this it is what makes it possible for higher psychical activities, scientific, artistic or ideological, to play such an important part in civilized life" (Freud 1930a, p. 97).

Much could be said about sublimation, which was the subject of study in the 65th *Congrès des psychanalystes de langue française* (2005) [the congress of francophone psychoanalysts], and which is, in my opinion, the result of arduous psychic work. When I say work, I refer particularly to the relationship between two persons, patient–analyst, in which psychic realities are woven in an actualisation of the past which contains childhood sexual desires. The work of mourning over being loved in exclusivity, the work of melancholia because it contains the narcissistic investitures which we cannot part with, the work on guilt originating in the sadism–masochism interplay. I think this work on guilt is the most important problem of cultural evolution, highlighting the fact that the price paid for the progress of culture lies in the loss of happiness due to the enhancement of the feeling of guilt.

This leads to an inevitable question: if civilisation is a product of human relations in all their complexity, can that which man has created turn against him?

However, "the relation of love to civilization loses its unambiguity", Freud continues, "On the one hand, love comes into opposition to the interests of civilization; on the other, civilization threatens love with substantial restrictions" (1930a, p. 103).

Another question arises: how does the process of civilisation originate? According to Freud, we can set our minds at rest only if we say that the cultural process is the particular modification undergone by the life process under the influence of a task set before it by Eros and stimulated by Ananke, external necessity, and this task is that of uniting single human beings into a larger unity with libidinal attachments between them. When, however, we compare the cultural process in humanity with the process of development or upbringing, we can conclude without much hesitation that the two are very similar in nature, if not, in fact, the same process applied to a different kind of object.

Man, civilisation, suffering, psychic pain, internal world, external world, relations, violence, pleasure, but, above all, love, whether in the form of beauty or of desire for exchange—I think we can only admire the wisdom of this man who, often accused of being obsolete and outdated, has simply changed the course of history.

To conclude, and as a homage to that great creator, Sigmund Freud, I will recall Plotinus VI 7 (38), who, following Plato, distinguishes a three-stage ascent of the soul to the Good. The soul recognises the beauty of sensible things and elevates itself towards the Good, which is beauty without form, beyond formal beauty, but, since beauty is linked to love, and love seeks invisible light, between the two they generate visible beauty.

There is no beauty more real than that of the wisdom we perceive in another person. Although we might find his or her face ugly (according to individual taste), if we seek the inner beauty that illuminates, we can ignore the external appearance.

Eros, "Heavenly Power"

The last, but certainly not the least important, of the characteristic features of civilization remains to be assessed: the manner in which the relationships of men to one another, their social relationships, are regulated – relationships which affect a person as a neighbour, as a source of help, as another person's sexual object, as a member of a family and of a State. (Freud, 1930a, pp. 94–95)

We recognize, then, that countries have attained a high level of civilization if we find that in them everything which can assist in the exploitation of the earth by man and in his protection against the forces of nature – everything, in short, which is of use to him – is attended to and effectively carried out. (Freud, 1930a, p. 92)

Beauty, cleanliness and order obviously occupy a special position among the requirements of civilization. (Freud, 1930a, p, 93)

What makes itself felt in a human community as a desire for freedom may be their revolt against some existing injustice, and so may prove favourable to a further development of civilization; it may remain compatible with civilization. But it may also spring from the remains of their original personality, which is still untamed by civilization and may thus become the basis in them of hostility to civilization. (Freud, 1930a, p. 96)

Here, we may put forward the hypothesis that fanaticism represents an obstacle for culture, a restraint, and even an aggression against it.

Sublimation of instinct is an especially conspicuous feature of cultural development; it is what makes it possible for higher psychical activities, scientific, artistic or ideological, to play such an important part in civilized life. If one were to yield to a first impression, one would say that sublimation is a vicissitude which has been forced upon the instincts entirely by civilization. But it would be wiser to reflect upon this a little longer. (Freud, 1930a, p. 97)

Man finds by experience that sexual (genital) love affords him his greatest gratification, so that it becomes in effect, the prototype of all happiness. However, there are a "small minority" who,

make themselves independent of their object's acquiescence by displacing what they mainly value from being loved onto loving; they protect themselves against loss of the object by directing their love, not to single objects but to all men alike; and they avoid the uncertainties and disappointments of genital love by turning away from its sexual aim and transforming the instinct into an impulse with an *inhibited aim*. (Freud, 1930a, p. 102)

But in the course of development the relation of love to civilization loses its unambiguity. On the one hand love comes into opposition to the interests of civilization; on the other, civilization threatens love with substantial restrictions. (1930a, p. 103)

So far, we can quite well imagine a cultural community consisting of double individuals like this, who, libidinally satisfied in themselves, are connected with one another through the bonds of common work and common interests. If this were so, civilization would not have to withdraw any energy from sexuality. (1930a, p. 108)

I think I can now hear a dignified voice admonishing me: 'It is precisely because your neighbour is not worthy of your love, and is on the contrary your enemy, that you should love him as yourself.' I then understand that the case is one like that of *Credo quia absurdum*.

Now it is very probable that my neighbour, when he is enjoined to love me as himself, will answer exactly as I have done and will repel me for the same reasons. I hope he will not have the same objective grounds for doing so, but he will have the same idea as I have. Even so, the behaviour of human beings shows differences, which ethics, disregarding the fact that such differences are determined, classifies as 'good' or 'bad'. So long as these undeniable differences have not been removed, obedience to high ethical demands entails damage to the aims of civilization, for it puts a positive premium on being bad. (Freud, 1930a, p. 111)

I once discussed the phenomenon that it is precisely communities with adjoining territories, and related to each other in other ways as well, who are engaged in constant feuds and in ridiculing each other – like the Spanish and Portuguese, for instance, the North Germans and South Germans, the English and Scotch, and so on. I gave this phenomenon the name of 'the narcissism of minor differences', a name which does not do much to explain it. (Freud, 1930a, p. 114)

That others should have shown, and still show, the same attitude of rejection surprises me less. For 'little children do not like it' when there is talk of the inborn human inclination to 'badness', to aggressiveness and destructiveness, and so to cruelty as well. (Freud, 1930a, p. 120)

If [a person] loses the love of another person upon whom he is dependent, he also ceases to be protected from a variety of dangers. Above all, he is exposed to the danger that this stronger person will show his superiority in the form of punishment. . . . A great change takes place only when the authority is internalized through the establishment of a super-ego. The phenomena of conscience then reach a higher stage. Actually, it is not until now that we should speak of conscience or a sense of guilt. (Freud, 1930a, p. 125)

The cultural super-ego has developed its ideals and set up its demands. Among the latter, those which deal with the relations of human beings to one another are comprised under the heading of ethics. (Freud, 1930a, p. 142)

The fateful question for the human species seems to me to be whether and to what extent their cultural development will succeed in mastering the disturbance of their communal life by the human instinct of aggression and self-destruction. It may be that in this respect precisely the present time deserves a special interest. Men have gained control over the forces of nature to such an extent that with their help they would have no difficulty in exterminating one another to the last man. They know this, and hence comes a large part of their current unrest, their unhappiness and their mood of anxiety. And now it is to be expected that the other of the two 'Heavenly Powers', eternal Eros, will make an effort to assert himself in the struggle with his equally immortal adversary. But who can foresee with what success and with what result? (Freud, 1930a, p. 145)

To conclude we might ask ourselves: is it the illusion of a future? Or is it the future of an illusion?

Who can foresee that, with what success and with what result?

NOTES

1. I am including an example derived from my personal experience which I have modified in such a way as to avoid the identification of any particular person, much in the same fashion as in the film industry, when they state that "any resemblance to real-life events or persons here depicted is pure coincidence".
2. Here, we should recall the three kinds of regressions (in the psychic temporality) as described by Freud: "topical", "temporal", and "formal" (1900a).
3. Taken from Geoffrey Hill's translation of Brand's agonised cry: "Tabets alt din Vinding skabte, Evigt ejes kun det tabte! (Ibsen, 1996, p. 118).
4. Some of the material in this chapter has been taken from my article, "Las raíces de la intolerancia" [The roots of intolerance], published in *El rapto de Europa. Crítica de la Cultura*, 2, May 2003.
5. Translator's note: Stefan Zweig's 1936 work, *Castellio gegen Calvin oder Ein Gewissen gegen die Gewalt* (published in English under the title *The Right to Heresy: Castellio against Calvin*) was, however, published in French and Spanish as *Conscience contre Violence* and *Conciencia contra la Violencia*, respectively, both of which translate into English as "Conscience against violence".

6. The following sections are based on a lecture of the same title, which I delivered at the University of Alcalá de Henares in 2000, and which has been modified for inclusion in this book.
7. Although edited, part of this chapter was excerpted from the article "Respect and dignity in psychoanalysis", published in the *Magazine of the Madrid Psychoanalytical Association (APM)*, 26 in 1997.
8. I say "translated" because, having no knowledge of the German language but suspecting that the term "discontents" is not quite the right one, I can only propose the title of "Civilization and its Well-being".

REFERENCES

Acuña Bermúdez, E. A. (2008). Psicoanálisis de la guerra, el conflicto armado y terrorismo. *Revista de Psicoanálisis, Psicoterapia y Salud Mental, 1*(5). Available at: http://psi.usal.es/rppsm/pdfn5/psicoanalisis delaguerraelconflictoarmadoyterrismo.pdf.

Al Aswany, A. (2012). Quoted in an article by *The Reader Online* dated August 17, 2012: http://thereaderonline.co.uk/2012/08/17/readers-of-the-world-egypt/.

Anzieu, D. (1989). *The Skin Ego*, C. Turner (Trans.). New Haven, CT: Yale University Press.

Anzieu, D. (1993). Autistic phenomena and the skin ego. *Psychoanalyic Inquiry, 13*: 42–48.

Aquinas, T. (2007)[1276]. *Summa Theologica, Volume 1, Part 1*, The Fathers of the English Dominican Province (Trans.). New York: Cosimo.

Armengol Millans, R. (2008). El fanatismo, una perversión del narcisismo. Sobre el origen y la acción del superyó, reflexiones morales. *Psicoanálisis: Revista de la Asociación Psicoanalítica Colombiana, 20*(1): 11–36.

Barnes, J. (2013). *The Pre-Socratic Philosophers*. London: Routledge.

Baricco, A. (2004) *An Iliad: A Story of War*. Edinburgh: Canongate, 2007.

Bassols, R. (1999). Sobre fanatismo y violencia. *Vol. IV. Sociedad Española de Psicoanálisis*.

Bateson, G. (1972). *Steps to an Ecology of Mind: Collected Essays in Anthropology, Psychiatry, Evolution and Epistemology*. San Francisco, CA:

Chandler and Aylesbury [reprinted Chicago: University of Chicago Press, 2000].

Bettelheim, B. (1950). *Love is not Enough: The Treatment of Emotionally Disturbed Children.* New York: Free Press [reprinted New York: Collier Books,1968].

Burton, R. (1621). *The Anatomy of Melancholy.* Printed for Henry Cripps: Oxford [reprinted New York: Tudor, 1921].

Calvin, J. (1536). *Institutes of the Christian Religion,* F. L. Battles (Trans.). Grand Rapids: William. B. Eerdmans, 1986.

Camus, A. (1953). *The Rebel,* A. Bower (Trans.). London: Hamish Hamilton [reprinted London: Penguin Books in association with Hamish Hamilton, 2000].

Chasseguet-Smirgel, J. (1990). On acting out. *International Journal of Psychoanalysis, 71:* 77–86.

Chasseguet-Smirgel, J. (2001). The ego ideal today: the triumph of the short way over the long way. Accessed at: www.epfeu.org.

Cheng, F. (2006). *The Way of Beauty: Five Meditations for Spiritual Transformation,* J. Gladding (Trans.). Vermont: Inner Traditions, 2009.

Cleckley, H. M. (1941). *The Mask of Sanity: An Attempt to Clarify Some Issues about the So-Called Psychopathic Personality* [reprinted 1998, 2011 Whitefish [Montana]: Literary Licensing, LLC].

Cosnier, J. (1989). Interacciones en la vida cotidiana. In: Utrilla Robles, M., Lebovici, S., & Cosnier, J. *Interacciones terapéuticas: Fronteras psicoanaliticas.* Madrid: Tecnipublicaciones.

David, C. (1974). A discussion of the paper by René Major on 'The Revolution of Hysteria'. *International Journal of Psychoanalysis, 55:* 393–395.

De Mijolla A. (1981). *Les visiteurs du moi* [The ego's visitors]. Paris: Les Belles Lettres (2nd edn, 1986). Summary in English in "Unconscious identification fantasies and family prehistory" (1987) *International Journal of Psychoanalysis, 68:* 397–403.

Dostoevsky, F. (1869). *The Idiot,* D. McDuff (Trans.). New York: Penguin Classics, 2004.

Etchegoyen, R. H. (1999). *Fundamentals of Psychoanalytical Technique.* London: Karnac [reprinted 2005].

Fain, M. (1966). Regression et psychosomatique. *Revue Française de Psychanalyse, 30:* 451–456.

Fain, M. (1982). *Le désir de l'interpréte.* Montagne: Aubier.

Foulkes, S. H. (1975). *Group Analytical Psychotherapy: Methods and Principles.* London: Gordon & Breach [reprinted London: Karnac, 2012].

Freud, S. (1895d). *Studies on Hysteria. S.E.*, *2*. London: Hogarth.

Freud, S. (1900a). *The Interpretation of Dreams. S.E. 4–5*. London: Hogarth.

Freud, S. (1912–1913). *Totem and Taboo. S.E.*, *13*. London: Hogarth.

Freud, S. (1916–1917). *Introductory Lectures on Psycho-Analysis. S.E.*, *16*: London: Hogarth.

Freud, S. (1919a). Lines of advance in psycho-analytic therapy. *S.E.*, *17*: 157–168. London: Hogarth.

Freud, S. (1920g). *Beyond the Pleasure Principle. S.E.*, *18*: 7–64. London: Hogarth.

Freud, S. (1921c). *Group Psychology and the Analysis of the Ego. S.E.*, *18*: 67–143. London: Hogarth.

Freud, S. (1923b). *The Ego and the Id. S.E.*, *19*: 3–66. London: Hogarth.

Freud, S. (1930a). *Civilization and its Discontents. S.E.*, *21*: 59–145. London: Hogarth.

Fromm, E. (1942). *The Fear of Freedom*. London: Routledge and Kegan Paul [reprinted London: Routledge Classics, 2001].

Gansel, D. (dir.) (2008). *The Wave* (*Die Welle*). Film. Momentum Pictures.

Gómez Esteban, R. (1997). Una perspectiva histórica de la psicoterapia de grupo. In: *Grupos terapéuticos y asistencia pública. Asociación Española de Neuropsiquiatría* (pp. 9–38). Barcelona: Paidós.

Gressot, M. (1953). Le mythe dogmatique et le système moral des Manichéens: essai psychanalytique. *Revue française de psychanalyse*, *17*(4): 398–427.

Gressot, M. (1979). *Le royaume intermédiaire*. Paris: Fil Rouge, Editions Presses Universitaires de France.

Hare, R. D., Hart, S. D., & Harpur, T. J. (1991). Psychopathy and the DSM-IV criteria for antisocial personality disorder. *Journal of Abnormal Psychology*, *100*: 391–398.

Ibsen, H. (1866). *Brand*, G. Hill (Trans.). London: Heinemann, 1978 [reprinted London: Penguin, 1996].

James, M., & Jongeward, D. (1971). *Born to Win: Transactional Analysis with Gestalt Experiments*. Reading, MA: Addison-Wesley, 1996.

Javaloy, F. (1984). *Introducción al Estudio del Fanatismo*. Barcelona: Edicions Universitat Barcelona.

Jones, R. (1976). The third wave. In: *No Substitute for Madness: A Teacher, His Kids, and the Lessons of Real Life*. Washington, DC: Island Press, 1981.

King, L. W. (Trans.) (2007). *Enuma Elish: The Epic of Creation*. New York: Filiquarian.

Kirk, G. S. (1954). *Heraclitus, the Cosmic Fragments: A Critical Study*. New York: Cambridge University Press [reprinted with corrections, 1962].

Klein, M. (1933). The early development of conscience in the child. In: *Love, Guilt and Reparation and Other Works, 1921–1945 (The Writings of Melanie Klein, Volume 1)* (pp. 248–258). London: Melanie Klein Trust, 1975 [reprinted New York: Simon & Schuster, 1999].

Klein, M. (1935). A contribution to the psychogensis of manic-depressive states. *International Journal of Psychoanalysis, 16*: 145–174. Reprinted in: *Love, Guilt and Reparation and Other Works, 1921–1945 (The Writings of Melanie Klein, Volume 1* (pp. 262–290). London: Melanie Klein Trust, 1975 [reprinted New York: Simon & Schuster, 1999].

Klein, M. (1946). Notes on some schizoid mechanisms. In: *Envy and Gratitude and Other Works 1946–1963 (The Writings of Melanie Klein, Volume 3)* (pp. 1–25). London: Hogarth Press, 1975 [reprinted London: Vintage, 1997].

Klein, M. (1955). On identification. In: *Envy and Gratitude and Other Works, 1946–1963 (The Writings of Melanie Klein, Volume 3)* (pp. 141–176). London: Hogarth Press, 1975 [reprinted London: Vintage, 1997].

Klein, M. (1957). Envy and gratitude. In: *Envy and Gratitude and Other Works 1946–1963 (The Writings of Melanie Klein, Volume 3)* (pp. 176–236). London: Hogarth Press, 1975 [reprinted London: Vintage, 1997].

Kohut, H. (1971). *The Analysis of the Self: A Systematic Approach to the Psychoanalytic Treatment of Narcissistic Personality Disorders*. New York: International Universities Press [reprinted Chicago, IL: University of Chicago Press, 2011].

Mahler, M. (1967). On human symbiosis and the vicissitudes of individuation. *Journal of the American Psychoanalytical Association, 15*: 740–763.

McDougall, J. (1989). *Theatres of the Body: Psychoanalytic Approach to Psychosomatic Illness*. New York: W.W. Norton.

Montaigne, M. de (2004). *The Essays: A Selection*, M. A. Screech (Trans.). London: Penguin.

Morin, E. (1977). *Method: Towards a Study of Humankind. Vol.1, The Nature of Nature*, J. L. Roland Bélanger (Trans.). New York: Peter Lang, 1992.

Neruda, P. (1924). *Twenty Love Poems and a Song of Despair*, W. S. Merwin (Trans.). London: Cape, 1969 [reprinted London: Penguin, 2007].

Nitsun, M. (2000). The future of the group. *International Journal of Group Psychotherapy, 50(4)*: 455–472.

Oz, A. (2006). *How to Cure a Fanatic. Israel and Palestine: Between Right and Right*. Princeton, NJ: Princeton University Press [reprinted London: Vintage Books, 2012].

Perdigao, G. (2007). The dark side of our Freudian inheritance. Article published online at International Psychoanalysis: http://international

psychoanalysis.net/2007/04/20/the-dark-side-of-our-freudian-inheritance-by-gunther-perdigao/.

Pichon Rivière, E. (1987). *Del Psicoanálisis a la Psicología social.* Buenos Aires: Editorial Nueva Visión.

Plotinus VI 7 (38). On how the multitude of forms came into being, and on the Good. In: L. P. Gerson (Ed.) (1996) *The Cambridge Companion to Plotinus.* Cambridge: Cambridge University Press [reprinted with corrections, Cambridge: Cambridge University Press, 1999].

Rangell, L. (1974). A psychoanalytic perspective leading currently to the syndrome of the compromise of integrity. *International Journal of Psychoanalysis, 55:* 3–12.

Rodríguez Daimiel, G. (1996). El tejedor de palabras: metáfora de la identidad psicoanalítica – V Simposio de la Asociación Psicoanalítica de Madrid: la identidad psicoanalítica, Madrid 23–24 de noviembre de 1996. *Revista de Psicoanálisis, 1997, extra:* 145–150.

Russell, B. (1910)(1973). The theory of logical types. In: D. Lackey (Ed.) (1973) *Russell, Essays in Analysis* (pp. 215–252). London: George Allen & Unwin.

Scheidlinger S. (1988). El concepto de regresión en la psicoterapia de grupo. In: M. Kiessen, (Ed.), *Dinámica de Grupo y Psicoanálisis de Grupo.* Mexico City: Editorial Limusa.

Sor, D., & Senet de Gazzano, M. R. (1993). *Fanatismo.* Buenos Aires: Ananké [reprinted Buenos Aires: Ediciones Biebel, 2010].

Strasser, T. (1981). *The Wave.* Logan (IA): Perfection Learning [reprinted New York: Random House, 2013].

Utrilla Robles, M. (1994). La infancia y la vejez. Correlaciones psicoanalíticas. *La Revista de APM (Asociacion Psicoanalitica de Madrid), 20*(94): 69–82.

Utrilla Robles, M. (1996). Confusión y elaboración: reflexiones psicoanalíticas sobre El misterio del solitario de J. Gaarder. *La Revista de la APM (Asociación Psicoanalítica de Madrid), 24*(96): 215–235.

Utrilla Robles, M. (1997). El respeto y la dignidad en la ética psicoanalítica. *Revista de Psicoanálisis de la Asociación Psicoanalítica de Madrid (APM), 26:* 177–200.

Utrilla Robles, M. (1998). *¿Son posibles las terapias en las Instituciones? Estudio Situacional.* Madrid: Biblioteca Nueva.

Utrilla Robles, M. (2000). Group psychology, individual psychology: a hymn to freedom. Lecture delivered at the University of Alcalá de Henares, Spain.

Utrilla Robles, M. (2003). Las raíces de la intolerancia. *El rapto de Europa. Crítica de la Cultura, 2:* 35–46.

Utrilla Robles, M. (2010). *Convulsiones en las Instituciones Psicoanaliticas I: Psicoanálisis y Psicoterapia*. Madrid: El Duende.

Utrilla Robles, M., & García Valdecasas, J. (1994). Psicosomática, obsesión y homosexualidad. *Revista de psicoterapia y psicosomática, 30–31*: 23–36.

Utrilla Robles, M., Lebovici, S., & Cosnier, J. (1989). *Interacciones terapéuticas: Fronteras psicoanalíticas*. Madrid: Tecnipublicaciones.

Von Berger, A. (1896). Review of Breuer and Freud's *Studien über Hysterie*. *Neue Freie Presse, 2*(2): xv.

Weber, M. (1905). *The Protestant Ethic and the Spirit of Capitalism*, S. Kalberg (Trans.). New York: Oxford University Press, 2011.

Winnicott, D. W. (1965a). *The Maturational Processes and the Facilitating Environment: Studies in the Theory of Emotional Development*. London: Hogarth Press.

Winnicott, D. W. (1965b). Ego distortion in terms of true and false self. In: *The Maturational Processes and the Facilitating Environment: Studies in the Theory of Emotional Development*. London: Hogarth Press.

Winnicott, D. W. (1971). *Playing and Reality*. London: Tavistock [reprinted London: Routledge, 2005].

Yalom, I. D. (1986). *Teoría y Práctica de la Psicoterapia de Grupo*. Mexico City: Fondo de Cultura Económica.

Zweig, S. (1936). *The Right to Heresy: Castellio against Calvin*, E. Paul & C. Paul (Trans.). London: Cassell.

INDEX

For Product Safety Concerns and Information please contact our EU representative GPSR@taylorandfrancis.com Taylor & Francis Verlag GmbH, Kaufingerstraße 24, 80331 München, Germany

Batch number: 08153785

Printed by Printforce, the Netherlands